You and Your Aging Parent

You and Your Aging Parent

The Practical Side of Love

Jill A. Boughton

GREENLAWN PRESS

ISBN 0-937779-28-8.
Library of Congress Card Catalog Number 93-81292.

Excerpts from Scripture are taken from the *New American Bible Old Testament* copyright © 1970; the *Revised New Testament of the New American Bible* copyright © 1986, and the *Revised Psalms of the New American Bible* copyright © 1991 by the Confraternity of Christian Doctrine Inc., 3211 Fourth Street, N.E., Washington, D.C. 20017-1194 and are used with permission. All rights reserved.

Copyright © 1994 by Jill A. Boughton. All rights reserved. Except for brief quotations in critical articles or reviews, no part of this book may be reproduced in any manner without prior permission. Write to Greenlawn Press, 107 South Greenlawn, South Bend, IN 46617.

99 98 97 96 95 94   5 4 3 2 1

Printed in the United States of America.

Contents

Introduction *vii*
1. My Parents Are Growing Older; What's That Like for Them? *1*
2. God's Plan *11*
3. Practical Advice in Caring for Parents *25*
4. Growth in Understanding *35*
5. Where Should They Live? *51*
6. Welcoming a Parent into Your Home *71*
7. Caring for a Parent in Other Living Situations *93*
8. Caring for a Parent with Disabilities *107*
9. Dying, Death and Grieving *127*
10. Preparing for My Own Aging and Death *141*

Introduction

Have your parents suddenly begun to show their age? Do you wonder what lies ahead for them and whether you will be called on to care for them in new ways? Perhaps you've seen magazine articles about the so-called sandwich generation — those who are weighing the needs of aging parents and the needs of children still living at home. Or perhaps your parents are still living, while you've already reached retirement age yourself. Instead of the anticipated leisure of retirement, you face new challenges in caring for them.

As medical advances enable people to live longer, more and more adult children are facing the question of how best to care for their aging parents or grandparents. In 1900, only one in 10 couples between 40 and 60 had one or more parents still alive. By 1990, over half had at least two parents alive. The fastest-growing age group within the U.S. population is the over-100 group!

Many of these survivors are strong and resilient, but medical technology has prolonged life for many people whose illnesses were almost always fatal in previous generations. Today, many older people must cope with multiple health problems. Over 86 percent of the elderly have some form of chronic illness. Over five percent of those between 60 and 80 and nearly 30 percent of those over 80 are affected by Alzheimer's disease alone. Longevity also makes it easier for people to outlive their financial provisions for old age.

Many books and magazine articles, workshops and seminars offer practical advice to caregivers. Some of these resources are very helpful.

However, I often find the current advice on my role as a caregiver disappointing. Many voices urge me to assert myself, to protect my time and energy and to avoid burnout. As necessary as these cautions may be, they omit the most important

You and Your Aging Parent

advice — to love my parents and lay down my life unconditionally for them.

Many in our society speak against such generous love. They say that I am wasting my precious time and talents on people who are no longer contributing members of society. They imply that those who can no longer achieve success have ceased to have value. Even more strident voices urge those who are old or infirm to end their own lives, with the collaboration of their physicians and their children.

The scriptural perspective is quite different. God alone gives life and takes it away, and every human being he has created is infinitely precious to him.

People may lose everything else — their ability to speak, to move, to control bodily functions — but they don't have to lose their dignity! By God's grace, we can respect them to the very end, when he decides it is time for their lives here to end.

Scripture is very clear about our lifetime obligation to our parents. In Ephesians, St. Paul refers all the way back to the Ten Commandments: " 'Honor your father and mother' is the first commandment to carry a promise with it — 'that it may go well with you, and that you may have long life on the earth' " (6:2–3).

The writer of Sirach advises, "My son, take care of your father when he is old; grieve him not as long as he lives. Even if his mind fail, be considerate with him. . . . For kindness to a father will not be forgotten. . . . A blasphemer is he who despises his father" (3:12–16) and "With your whole heart honor your father; your mother's birthpangs forget not. Remember, of these parents you were born; what can you give them for all they gave you?" (7:27–28).

Jesus rebukes those who refuse to support their parents, especially those who use religion as an excuse for neglecting this duty. (See Matthew 15:3–6, Mark 7:9–13.)

St. Paul counsels Timothy about children's duties toward aging parents and widows. He says children have primary responsibility in this matter; the church should step in only when there are no children or grandchildren. "If a widow has any children or grandchildren, let these learn that piety begins at home and that they should fittingly support their parents and

Introduction

grandparents; this is the way God wants it to be. . . . If anyone does not provide for his own relatives and especially for members of his immediate family, he has denied the faith; he is worse than an unbeliever" (1 Tm. 5:4, 8).

Personally, I've experienced the scriptural obligation to love, honor and care for my parents not as an imposition or an irritation but as an invitation, an invitation to share Christ's love, to grow in holiness and to prepare those I love to be with him forever. My heavenly Father has a plan for me as well as for those I love. It's a harmonious plan, not one in which my needs conflict with the needs of my parents. He promises that his burden is light and that he and I are yoked together in bearing it. I've found this to be absolutely true.

During our wedding ceremony, the priest asked my husband and me if we had come freely and without reservation to give ourselves to each other in marriage. The words "freely and without reservation" express the way I want to love not only my husband but my parents and children as well.

My husband bikes several miles to work each day. He says that welcoming his mother into our home was a little like riding a bicycle in the rain. If you try to protect yourself from getting even slightly wet, you will end up frustrated and angry. On the other hand, if you accept the fact that you are going to get wet whatever you do and settle into the experience, you may even enjoy it. Likewise, if we set aside 10 hours a week to care for Mom, we are likely to be resentful if unforeseen circumstances require even an extra half-hour. On the other hand, if we commit ourselves wholeheartedly to loving her, whatever it takes, we give God a blank check. Sometimes we feel as if our account is overdrawn, but we have also frequently discovered that God has deposited unimagined resources on which we can draw.

Of course, I don't always achieve this ideal — to care for my mother-in-law "without reservation." God could have entrusted her to angels, but he planned for us weak human beings to take care of one another, drawing on his strength. Because I'm no angel, I try not to be too shocked when I find myself exhausted, baffled, irritated and otherwise inadequate in caring for those I love. Even if I weren't a selfish sinner, I couldn't care for Mom perfectly. If I could, she wouldn't need a divine Savior! God made her for himself, and he alone is the perfect Lover she desires.

Also, I'm not in this alone. As a member of the body of Christ, I can draw on the strength of many others. Together we can love our parents more fully than any of us could do on our own.

Good friends are a resource more helpful than books and seminars. In serving as a caregiver I've received tremendous support from other Christians in similar circumstances. They belong to a variety of denominations, yet they share the conviction that they are answering a call from God. Their parents have many different needs and circumstances, and they care for them in many different ways. Some of these parents live in nursing homes far from their children; some live in their children's homes. Despite these differences, we all have stories of similar challenges and of God's abundant grace. We can learn so much from one another!

This book draws on the experiences of many people, some of them caregivers and some on the receiving end. To respect everyone's privacy, I have changed their names and sometimes combined or modified their stories. However, all the wisdom contained in this book comes from real people in actual situations. I hope it will be both practical and inspiring to others.

Among those I have consulted are Mary Abella, Marylyn Barrett, Carolyn Bassett, Dawn Boardman, Sue Brennan, June Burke, Susan Busk, Jean Chambers, Harmony B. Cooper, Valerie Day, Patti Deakin, Jeanne DeCelles, Will and Vickie DeSanto, Lois Esselstrom, Nano Farabaugh, Linda Finke, Sister Elizabeth Grannan, S.P., Connie Hackenbruck, Thelma Hemple, Viola L. Jakiesz, Terry Kelly, Barbara Koller, Eva Kruse, Aletta J. Kuipers, Barb Little, Sandra Maichen, Janette Martin, Nancy McCue, Maureen McDonough, Foster and Lois McRell, Louise Minotti, Marie Misiewicz, Jane O'Malley, John F. and Mary R. Pajor, Pam Peterson, Mary Pingel, Ellie Peters, Margaret W. Pomelee, Barbara Ramsby, Dorothy Ranaghan, Pat Rath, Lucy Rathbun, Don and June Renaud, Eve Rhodes, Bud and Sharon Rose, Kathy Shoufler, Sharon Sklorenko, Eva Staffelbach, Marge Studer, Clara Thibeau, Elinor Thompson,

Introduction

Chris Urbanski, Bob and Adella Waymouth, Ruth Whitney and Mike Zengel.

My direct experience comes from sharing our home for the past two years with my mother-in-law, Henrietta Boughton, a stalwart 88-year-old. Throughout the book I refer to her as "Mom." Although she suffers from Alzheimer's disease, I heartily agree with a friend who said, "Someday I hope I can be as gracious an old lady as she is!" Besides my mother-in-law, our household includes my very supportive husband John and our six children, who range in age from four to 18.

Because most caregivers and 60 percent of those over age 65 are women, I have adopted the convention of using feminine pronouns to refer to both, except in cases where a story makes more sense if it refers to both parents or just to the father. I trust the reader will be able to apply this to parents of both sexes.

CHAPTER ONE

My Parents Are Growing Older; What's That Like for Them?

In one sense, this is a false question. Every individual ages differently and perceives her aging differently.

Most people never consciously think of themselves as old. They simply adapt their actions to physical changes and new limitations. For example, when their vision changes, they stop driving, or stop driving at night.

There really is no elderly personality as such. Elderly people are people, just older. Old age doesn't make sour people sweet or courteous people rude, unless there is also illness involved. Generally, older people retain the character traits they have spent their lifetime developing.

Here is an example given by one daughter.

"As Dad got older, he got more and more stubborn. All his life he declared that no one could ever tell him what to do. Only weeks before he died of lung cancer, he was still smoking. When my mother chided him, he said, 'Nobody has ever told me what to do and they're not going to start now!' To the end, he denied that his smoking had anything to do with the cancer; it was all a coincidence! He also never acknowledged that he might be facing death."

In Mom Boughton's case, the character which has endured

is quite different. As her Alzheimer's has progressed, she has forgotten how to do once-familiar tasks such as dressing herself and writing checks. However, she never forgets to express gratitude or to defer to others. She still practices lifetime habits of kindness, courtesy and prayer, which makes it a pleasure for us to take care of her physical needs.

Trish testifies, "I've enjoyed getting to know Mom better as a person in her own right. She's shared with me her memories of trivial as well as important events. I often wonder if I'm getting a glimpse of myself as I'll be in 25 years!"

Even though every individual ages differently, there are common threads to the experience of growing older. People experience changes that affect them physically, emotionally, socially and spiritually. Every person may not experience every one of these changes, but together they form a cluster of typical changes and reactions. Children need to be as understanding as possible about these changes.

My mother-in-law sometimes says, "You just don't understand! You don't understand what it's like to have trouble seeing, to shake all the time, to have trouble remembering the simplest things, to be old!"

Of course, she's right. I haven't experienced any of this, so in a sense I don't understand. I have to rely on what she says and what I observe. I try not to underestimate her pain and difficulty.

On the other hand, I, too, am a human being, and I have experienced similar things. I'm not blind, but I've tried to grope my way through unfamiliar places in the dark. I, too, have lost loved ones who were precious to me. I, too, am growing older. By God's grace, I can imagine what it's like for her.

It's also a good thing that I don't completely share her experience. Sometimes emotional distance helps me see what's going on and how her anxiety, grief or anger can hinder her from living the kind of life she really wants. Then I can help her judge the situation more objectively and take action to compensate for her weaknesses.

I do not contradict my mother-in-law. In a sense she is right, and I don't feel what she's feeling. So I sit down and say,

"Tell me about it. I do want to understand what it's like for you." After I've listened with my mind and my heart, I sometimes ask, "Can I suggest something that might help?"

One senior citizen advises younger people, "Let oldsters speak for themselves; don't assume you know what they're thinking." With this in mind, the following reflections on what it's like to grow older are mostly in the words of people who have passed age 65.

Perspectives on Aging

"Nothing stays the same. Society is changing so rapidly! Many of the things my generation took for granted seem to be up for grabs today."

"I find it hard to make decisions. There are so many factors to consider! I often postpone decisions, but that doesn't make things any clearer."

"We'd rather be independent; it's easier to do without than to ask for help. It's hard to admit we can no longer do things we've always done, like driving."

"With age, I've realized that certain things that used to have to be done aren't that important. I'm free to respond to someone's need without finishing some task first."

A 96-year-old widow who can't get out much anymore says simply, "As I've grown older, I have more time to notice flowers, birds and things around me."

This sense of priorities can be a gift to others. I bustle around accomplishing this and that while Mom sits in her chair dozing, reading a little, listening to music, watching birds at the hanging feeder and squirrels on the lawn.

One day she said to me, "Don't you ever get to sit down?" She wasn't chiding me, just noticing that something important was missing in all my activity. Realizing that I was too involved in nonessentials, I patted her hand and sat down for a little chat.

Mom doesn't do much of anything, yet she contributes so much to our household. Her presence in our home is a constant reminder to me that people and relationships should take priority over things and tasks.

Physical Changes

Even healthy older people usually experience some slowing down. They can't move as fast or squeeze as many things into a day or keep track of a full schedule.

"When you get older, you just slow down. This is hard for younger people to understand. Everything takes longer: eating, getting in and out of the car, everything. There are obvious reasons for it — we can't see or hear so well, we aren't as strong and we just tire more quickly."

"We have good days and bad days, and we can't predict them."

"It's easy to romanticize retirement. After working for 30 years, I began to look forward to retirement as a time of glorious freedom and activity. I planned to travel, take courses, write a book, plant a large garden, visit old friends, do volunteer work and develop new hobbies. Then, when I finally reached retirement age, I found that I didn't have enough energy to do so much. My goals were unrealistic. If I hadn't scaled them down, I might have become very bitter and frustrated."

Some seniors reach mental or emotional overload more rapidly than others. Some are still able to juggle multiple commitments while others are satisfied just to take care of their own needs each day and perhaps accomplish one additional task.

Aging is a little like going camping. When you're camping, ordinary things such as cooking and cleaning take much longer than they do at home. If you expect to whip through these tasks and get on to the fun activities of your vacation, you are likely to be very frustrated. However, if you see these tasks as a valuable part of the camping experience and enjoy them with your family, the days will be richer. Likewise, an older person may not accomplish much in an average day. Getting up, bathing and getting dressed, preparing meals and cleaning up, bringing in and sorting the mail, writing a letter or doing a little shopping quickly fill the day.

Younger people may not understand this. Most of us run on tight schedules that permit no slowing down.

Slowing down is hard on the older person, too. One senior

My Parents Are Growing Older

admits, "I used to be able to get a big job done in a day by running on high speed from morning till night. Now I have to rest several times or even take a nap, and it takes more than a day.

"As age has made me slower and more awkward, I've had to battle against pride and anger. I don't move fast and I'm not as much help in the kitchen as I used to be, but I resent it when I'm not allowed to help at all!

"On the other hand, I'm glad people don't expect as much of me and are willing to give me a little extra help."

With tongue in cheek, another senior comments on her physical limitations, "One advantage to growing older is that no one expects you to go on picnics anymore. I hate picnics!"

Mental Changes

Although older people possess a vast store of knowledge and experience, forgetfulness often puts what they have learned out of reach. Such mental abilities as calculation also tend to slow down. Perhaps the combination of knowledge and slowdown produces the kind of wisdom one senior expressed: "The most important thing I've learned since I passed 65 is that I don't have all the answers! I'm grateful; that means I still have a lot to learn!"

Nora says, "My mother knows so much! Sometimes I take a pen and a notepad, sit down beside her and ask her about what she knows. This includes stories about people and events from the past, but there is also a wealth of practical knowledge: how to shop for specific items, how to make repairs, how to cook, how to make things last longer. When I'm facing a decision, big or small, I try to remember to ask Mom for her input. Did she ever have to change doctors? How did she select a new one? How would she redecorate my office? Questions like these have unlocked wonderful stories and memories as well as a wealth of practical wisdom."

Regarding memory loss, a 79-year-old says, "I think my mind goes on vacation a great deal, especially when I'm trying to recall a name, place or other information that has been stored up there all these years."

How do people compensate?

One wife says, "Our memories aren't so good, so we have to write everything down on the calendar." Another woman confesses, "I'm slowing down mentally, so I don't push so hard on studying, reading, memorizing, etc. It's a lot more fun this way!"

Emotional Changes

An older person's senses or memory may fade, but that doesn't usually dull her feelings. She may be reticent about expressing strong feelings but that doesn't mean she doesn't have them.

Some people experience more emotional tranquillity as they age, while others say they are more sensitive or irascible. Here are some typical comments.

"I'm not so uptight."

"As we've grown older, we've become more peaceful and settled, but we do worry about our children's families and problems!"

"Some things bother me more than they used to."

"I have become more sensitive with age. What helps me, though, is remembering old times and God's blessings."

Grief may be a frequent companion as dear friends suffer and die. Losing a husband is particularly difficult. Two lives were woven together for so many years; suddenly the widow is alone in a new way.

"It can be depressing to realize I have reached the peak of the journey of life and now it's all downhill—maybe not so fast, but nevertheless downhill!"

Anger about what is happening to her and fear of what lies ahead are other common emotions.

"Growing old is frightening. You don't know what to expect."

Leah agrees. "My mother is so fearful. It isn't just because she's old—she's always been prone to anxiety and worry—but old age has intensified her fears and made ordinary events seem threatening."

My Parents Are Growing Older

Social Changes

Changes within the family can be especially hard on mothers. Liz says, "I built my life around my family, so it was hard for me to accept my children growing up and moving away. I still miss them!" Many women like Liz, who chose to be full-time mothers and didn't develop other interests, feel suddenly useless and bored when the children have all left the nest.

The older person's social world may shrink for two kinds of reasons, those which come from her and those which come from others. As she grows older, making new friends may seem like too much effort. She may be set in her ways, unwilling to compromise, and unconcerned with what others think of her. Some people seem more free to speak their minds as they grow older, and this can alienate acquaintances and be a strain even on the most tolerant friends. The older person's declining health, lack of mobility, poor vision or hearing can also limit social relationships. If she moves to a different town or even a different neighborhood, she may be reluctant to make new friends and unable to keep up with old ones.

Since the same things are probably happening to her old friends, staying in touch is doubly difficult. Younger friends, on the other hand, may be too busy — or seem to be too busy — to have time for older people.

Sometimes seniors experience prejudice and outright rejection. One couple says, "After we retired, many people no longer seemed interested in us beyond a cursory 'Hello.' The only people who remain 'interesting' are those with wealth or social status."

Another woman explains the difficulty from her side. "Because I move slowly, it's impossible to go to social affairs without holding others back from moving at the pace they prefer."

On the other hand, those willing to invest a little time and patience can find a wonderful treasure in the friendship of the elderly. They bring to a friendship a lifetime of observing, coping, creating and relating to others.

Older people have a pretty good idea what they can and cannot tolerate. On the one hand, they've successfully weathered many crises and they know they can cope. On the other hand, they know their limitations pretty well. They need the freedom to withdraw to a quieter place when there's too much noise and confusion, too many relationships, too many things demanding their attention. Their children may be doing them a favor by encouraging them to get out of the house, meet new people and try new things, but this can also be overwhelming and upsetting for the older person.

Andrea says, "My mother values her privacy and independence. This doesn't mean she doesn't value her many friendships and want to maintain them, but it has to be on her terms, according to her energy and her priorities.

"For example, she hasn't missed the weekly meeting of her bridge club in 30 years, but she has no interest in making new friends at our church's monthly meeting of seniors. I know it's going to be traumatic for her when one of those bridge partners dies or becomes incapacitated, but I can't discourage her from investing in them, nor would I want to.

"I try to introduce new people into her life, and I try to help her maintain contact with old friends. I also try to listen when she says, 'I'm just too tired to reach out to anyone today.' If she repeats that refrain too often, though, I suspect that she's depressed and not just tired. Reaching out to others has often pried me loose from self-concern, and I want Mother to have this opportunity, too. I keep trying to help her find the right balance."

Older people make comments like these:

"I like things neat and orderly!"

"I need quiet and rest. Younger people don't seem to understand this."

A perceptive daughter comments, "My mother has become quieter as she's grown older. At first I worried about her, but she doesn't seem to be withdrawing from life. She's aware of everything going on around her; she just doesn't feel the need to comment on it all! She can listen to someone else without needing to bring the conversation back to herself. This makes her a wonderful confidante. Her peacefulness is soothing and contagious.

"I think, too, that as Mom is beginning to withdraw from

sensory attachments her spirit is drawing closer to heaven. This helps me remember what does and doesn't have lasting value."

Spiritual Changes

Older people may lose interest in church activities or in spiritual reading, perhaps because of the physical, mental and social changes already mentioned. However, many experience a closer relationship with God and a deeper thirst to know him. This seems natural as they draw closer to the time when they will meet him face to face.

One couple reports, "Since retirement, we have more time for prayer. With a large family, there's always something to intercede for! We try to keep in touch with our children and grandchildren through letters and phone calls so we know what to pray for."

Another couple says, "As we've aged, we find ourselves spiritually seeking, searching, questioning and praying for guidance."

A widow says, "I've always been close to the church, but through the charismatic renewal the Holy Spirit became part of me, along with Jesus and God the Father. Now God is a close friend I can talk to anytime."

Ruth observes, "The older my mother gets, the closer to God she seems. She has always been a woman of prayer, but earlier in her life her many responsibilities sometimes crowded out the desire of her heart. Now that she has less to do, she really devotes herself to loving God and loving others. She never sits idle but always has a prayerbook in her hands. She writes down prayer requests and remembers them faithfully, often calling friends for updates on their needs. I know her arthritis causes her a great deal of pain, but I never hear her complain. Instead, I know she offers up her small sufferings for the salvation of others."

Older people who remain spiritually alive and growing show a deep trust in God. They may not always understand God's purposes for them — for example, why he has allowed them to suffer a chronic illness — but they do resist the temptation to lose hope or become bitter.

Cora expresses this well. "Spiritually, I hope I'm growing. To tell the truth, I can't see much progress. The Lord apparently can't either, since he hasn't called me home yet!

"I really don't know what the Lord has in mind for older people. There are a great many of us, so he must have some ideas!"

CHAPTER TWO

God's Plan

God has a "whole-life plan" for your parent, and he has a "whole-life plan" for you. You don't fully accomplish his plan in a single decisive instant but over a lifetime of choices. Your correct choices aim you in the right direction and your wrong choices can bring you to repentance, to forgiveness and to redirection.

God's plan is worked out in each unique individual, yet his goal for all of us is the same — to grow in loving union with him and with others. Every circumstance in our lives can either stimulate that growth or be an obstacle to it. The difference depends on our response.

For example, aging itself can be a way of drawing nearer to God in humble dependence and gratitude, or it can be a source of bitterness, complaint and rebellion against God's plan. Similarly, caring for a parent can be a way of serving Christ present in the least of his brothers, and growing like him in patience, love and fortitude, or it can be an occasion for resentment and anger.

Knowing God's plan for your parents helps clarify your own role. Sometimes I find it helpful to think of myself as my mother-in-law's spiritual bridesmaid. Not only am I trying to make her comfortable and happy here on earth, but, what matters far more, I am helping her prepare to be united forever with her Savior in heaven.

11

You and Your Aging Parent

My role in this is subsidiary. Jesus, the Bridegroom, has called Mom and made precious promises to her. It's up to her to respond to those promises and to do all she can to ready herself for the marriage.

However, there are things I can do to make sure everything is in order for the wedding. I can help her not get bogged down in the details of the preparation or in the inevitable delays and setbacks. I can encourage her, assuring her that she is precious and attractive to the Lord. I can gently urge her to let go of the things of this earth, the things that make her anxious so that she loses sight of the joyous certainty that one day she will be united with her heavenly bridegroom. I can help her to keep her spirit fresh and eager by sharing Scripture, music and prayer with her, taking her to church services, and encouraging conversation with others who are journeying toward the same goal.

Let's look more closely at God's plan and what can intervene to frustrate that plan.

I asked several people who are aging gracefully what special work God has for seniors and what advice they would give to their peers. Their wise words provide a window on God's plan.

"Live each day as if it were your last on earth."

"God wants us to intercede in prayer at all times. He wants us to set a good example. Keep praying that we can be guided by the Holy Spirit to say and do what God would like us to say and do."

"There are all kinds of volunteer work, classes in art and other things. Most of all, though, God's special volunteer work is for us to pray for the needs of others: for our family and friends, and for the world."

"Spiritually, I'm not in a time of such active service but a time for reading, studying and searching Scripture with expectant, eager faith, seeking to grow closer to God. At first I was hesitant about studying the Bible on my own, but I found several excellent Bible studies in my local Christian bookstore and chose one my pastor recommended."

God's Plan

Faith

These pieces of advice reflect faith in God and a desire to spend time with him in prayer.

Perhaps you'd like to pray with your parent but you've never done it before and it seems awkward. Here are some ways people have found to share their faith and to pray together.

Louise says, "Mother and I often pray together, each in her own way. When needs arise in the family, we recite the prayer that is most familiar to her, the rosary. When she's sick or I sense that she's worried or frightened, I pray in my own words. I don't pressure her to pray my way, but sometimes she surprises me by praying spontaneously from her heart."

Sherry has another suggestion. "I find a natural way to pray with someone is to watch a Christian television show like *The 700 Club*, hold her hand and pray along with the evangelist."

Even though my mother-in-law is often confused, she appreciates prayer. When I take her hand and begin the Lord's Prayer, I'm amazed how often she chimes in. Familiar prayers seem to comfort her a lot. She also likes to sing familiar hymns with me. It's wonderful to praise God together in song!

Not all parents are open to praying with others. For some, prayer is strictly a private activity. If your mother doesn't want you to pray aloud with her, be sure you continue to pray for her. One nursing-home chaplain observed that even people who claim to be agnostic usually don't object if she prays for them according to her own beliefs. She noted that people often have a strong belief in a higher power even though they don't consider themselves religious. Tactful questions can draw them out on the subject. "Where are you on your spiritual journey?" "Do you believe there is a power greater than yourself?" "What kind of funeral service would you like?"

It's not always possible to have spiritual conversations. Linda says, "I wish I had been able to talk with my mother on a different level as she was dying. I wanted to talk about her relationship with the Lord and encourage her to go to confession, but we never had that sort of conversation or relationship. We just didn't seem to be able to talk about spiritual things.

13

"I did get a priest to see her before she died, and I arranged for one of her friends to bring her Communion in the hospital every day. I prayed for her a lot, and I talked with a close friend. That helped me to be more peaceful as her death approached."

It's often easier for a parent to discuss spiritual things with a chaplain or a family friend. Of course, this should never be arranged without her permission.

Sometimes even the comfort of a past relationship with the Lord is missing. Anita says, "I witnessed to my mother, but I don't know how much she understood. Her faith was somewhat formal. She knew her catechism but didn't have a personal relationship with the Lord. I shared with her for hours and she seemed to be drinking it all in, but the next time we talked about it she acted as if nothing had registered. I did pray with her every night before she went to bed, and I can only trust that she felt the Lord's love through the way I cared for her."

A person who once professed a vibrant faith may express doubts, especially as her health declines. Arguing with her is seldom productive, but sometimes it helps to read Scripture aloud. We have found that doubts often dissolve as more love is given. Mom isn't really saying, "I don't believe in God"; she's saying something more like, "How can I be sure God loves me in the midst of all this pain and confusion?" Affectionate touches, with extra attention to her and to her physical needs, often help her over a hump like this.

Don't underestimate the power of prayer, either. Tina says, "My father didn't want to receive Communion, so the deacon asked if he could pray with us. After we prayed he asked Dad again if he wanted to receive Communion, and this time the answer was yes!

"I tried not to force religion on my dad, but before I left the hospital I always prayed the Lord's Prayer with him. Even if he was asleep, I said it aloud. It's a very precious memory."

What if your parent is an unbeliever, hostile to prayer or any expression of Christian faith? Laura says, "My father wouldn't allow expressions of affection or any discussion of Christian faith. I had to convince myself not to feel guilty about

God's Plan

this. Not all situations are ideal; we can only do what we can do."

It helps to remember that God loves your parent even more than you do and will give her opportunities for repentance and faith in ways you could not plan and may not even see. Pray faithfully for her. Communicate God's love in the way you care for her. Invite Christian friends who can share their faith in a friendly way to visit her. Be alert to the Spirit's guidance in what you say to her and what you do for her. Then leave the rest to God.

Trust

God wants his children to trust him in all things. Sometimes we think we have a better idea of what's best for ourselves or for others. When we try to take matters into our own hands, we get in over our heads. The result is often fear and anxiety because things don't go the way we planned or because the future is out of our control.

Older people, like younger people, can be anxious and fearful about many things: health, safety, finances and inability to care for themselves or to do what they used to do. Finally, all of us must face our most basic fear, the fear of death.

Scripture suggests a solution: "Perfect love casts out all fear" (1 Jn. 4:18).

It's fruitless to say, "Don't worry about that." She is worrying about it, and sheer willpower seldom dissolves worry. When Mom is fearful, I try to let her know I take her concern seriously. I give her as much specific evidence as possible that everything is being taken care of. For example, if she's worried about whether she paid a bill, I show her the receipt or canceled check. She may forget that she asked and need to see it several times before the matter is laid to rest.

Other worries are about less tangible things: Will I remember everyone's birthday? Will I be able to get to sleep? Why do I get mixed up so easily? These have no easy answers. I promise I will tell her when a birthday is coming up, that I have all these things written on my calendar. I try to reassure her with frequent hugs and touches, indicating that, whatever she does,

15

whatever happens to her, I love her and I am here for her. Over time, this has begun to heal the underlying fears, fear of being alone and fear of dying. Sometimes we can talk directly about these fears but they exist on a level much deeper than the rational mind. Prayer helps, Scripture helps, music helps, hugs help somehow to touch that deep level.

Some people are anxious about death itself. They may doubt the existence of God and heaven, or whether they will go there.

It's helpful if parents can discuss these fears with their children, perhaps with their pastor's assistance. Scripture gives many wonderful assurances of God's love for us and the place he has prepared for those who love him. Depending on a person's religious tradition, it may be good for her to receive sacramental reconciliation and anointing or to profess her faith aloud.

Many more people are afraid, not of death, but of dying. They don't want to die alone. They're afraid they won't be able to stand the pain, or that decisions about their care will be taken out of their hands.

Fears of dying may be very persistent, but most of them occur before the actual moment of death. A chaplain says, "In 12 years as a chaplain, I've met very few people who were actually afraid to die when the moment came. I've had to help them work through their feelings beforehand, and family members often need help in letting go, but the dying person is usually ready to die as soon as she is sure she's been reconciled with everyone in the family. At the moment of death, God gives the necessary courage."

Of course, there are no guarantees regarding how and when a person will die, but children can make comforting promises as long as they mean to keep them. "Please don't wait to phone me if you're afraid, even in the middle of the night." "We'll make sure someone from the family is with you in the hospital all the time." "I'm going to be right across the hall from your room; you can ring your bell whenever you need me." Even if the parent is unconscious, holding her hand may let her know she is not alone. Reading Scripture and singing familiar hymns are also very comforting.

Gratitude

Everyone enjoys being around an older person who is cheerful and grateful for God's many blessings in her life. In fact, people are sometimes surprised when they hear how many hardships an older person has endured. Far from embittering her, those hardships have only made her more grateful. When she looks back over her life, she fastens on God's mercies and sees his hand in the most severe trials.

She is grateful for the present as well as the past, knowing that God is still with her.

Rhoda says, "I try to accept life from God's hand, knowing that he's able to give me strength one day at a time for what he asks me to do."

Etta agrees, "Each day is a gift from God. Accept it as such and do whatever you can with the ability you have."

For Dorothy, this can be very difficult. "It's hard not feeling useful, but I try to be patient, pray, love my neighbor, witness to others and encourage others to build a good home life." This is plenty to keep her busy. She also suggests, "Try not to recite aches and pains, illnesses and operations. No one likes to listen to a complainer!"

It's depressing to be around someone who constantly complains and finds fault. This habit is hard to break, and arguing about the facts seldom produces a change of heart. It doesn't do much good to say "But look at all these wonderful things in your life!" when a person is intent on complaining about the hard things.

Nevertheless, God wants us to grow in gratitude so that we can receive his love more freely. What can you do if your mother seems stuck in a habit of complaining?

Try not to take criticism personally or feel guilty about everything that displeases your mother. While you should make every effort to please her, you won't always succeed, often through no fault of your own. A spouse or friend who isn't so close to the situation can help you avoid feeling guilty without cause.

In your own life, cultivate gratitude toward God and others, especially your mother. Tell your mother frequently how glad you are to be able to care for her, how grateful you are for the gift of life and the nurture she gave you.

Sometimes you will be able to shed new light on a situation that has embittered your mother, to help her see how much good has come out of it or how the people involved had good intentions despite the results. Such moments are gifts of grace. Take advantage of them when they arise, because they can't be prearranged.

Most of all, loving and caring for your mother day after day will create a secure environment where she can eventually let go of bitterness.

Sometimes it's guilt rather than complaining which blocks gratitude. The older person feels responsible for some past disaster and has never been able to forgive herself for it. One woman, for example, refused to loan her younger brother money; soon after that he committed suicide, and she still feels responsible for his death. In this case, she doesn't blame God but herself.

Her children let her talk about this as often as she wants. It starts out as the same old story, but occasionally something she says sheds new light on what actually happened. For example, she may admit that her brother was already troubled and confused before he asked her for money. As they talk with their mother, they pray that God himself will assure her that he forgives her.

Learning

Many seniors talk about how very important it is to keep learning.

Joanna says, "Keep learning at every stage of your life. Stretch your mind as much as you can. If you aren't learning and there are no demands on you, your toes curl up. I keep fighting that!"

She adds, "I also try to stay involved and active politically. I encourage friends to register to vote. I write often to local, state and national officials on subjects I feel strongly about and understand firsthand. I make sure I always get my facts straight so I don't embarrass myself or mislead others."

God's Plan

Several things will work against remaining mentally alert. Physical difficulties can make it hard for a person to get out to events in the community, to see the small print in the newspaper or to hear the radio. Where there is a will, however, there is usually a way. The law requires public buildings and programs to be accessible to those with handicaps. Many libraries provide tapes of music or readings from current periodicals for those who are blind.

A more serious obstacle is the older person's disinterest or unwillingness to keep stretching her mind. She may be realistic in thinking she can't learn anything new. On the other hand, you may be able to pick up clues about things that still hold some interest for her and follow up on those interests.

Love

God loves us and he wants us to remain connected with others. He wants us to feel his love through others' hands and feet, minds and voices, and to communicate his love to others in the same ways. Those who stay close to him will find themselves reaching out to others in love, even though they may not be able to do as much for others as they once could.

This can be a difficult adjustment. Those who are used to taking care of others in active ways may feel they are loving less if all they can do is pray for others, encourage them or write them upbeat notes. They need to be told how much these acts of kindness are appreciated.

Joanna shares her secrets for loving others. "I try to be happy about being a senior citizen. I read Scripture a lot, underlining passages I find encouraging. Instead of thinking about myself, I make it a point to encourage friends and family members. I tell them how much I delight in them! I try to mention specific things they've done to hearten me. I schedule time daily to phone others and chat."

Retirement can stir up temptations to selfishness. It requires a balance between taking proper care of yourself while still being generous toward others. The Martins have found that balance. "We were so busy raising our children we didn't have a chance to do everything we wanted to do for ourselves.

19

Now that we're retired we can do some of those things, but we try to think of others first, just as we always have. That's what life is all about! Doing for others makes us happy."

It's a challenge for older people to relate to younger ones. Nola says, "I don't try to advise younger people. I ask about their interests and try to see things from their viewpoint, relate to them on their level and answer their questions. I do not judge."

Margaret points out that understanding is a mutual project. "Younger people need to understand that we were brought up in a different age with different values. We really appreciate it, for example, when a young man opens a door for a woman or an older person. On the other hand, we try to understand that our grandchildren are growing up in a different world, too — different music, language, habits, dress and a lot of peer pressure we didn't have to deal with."

Briege recounts how well her mother relates to her grandchildren. "Mom is behind her grandchildren 100 percent. It hurts her when the toddler stumbles and falls. She softly points out to me when he has fallen asleep or is absorbed in 'reading' a book. She notices when the older children have grown, styled their hair differently or taken other pains with their appearance. She always compliments them and their parents when the children take time to do something kind for her. She's proud of their accomplishments and believes in them even when we parents find them exasperating. 'He's a good boy,' she'll say, 'he's just testing you right now.' 'He's grown so fast, it must be awkward for him to handle that big body.' 'She's so pretty, no wonder she spends a lot of time in front of the mirror!' "

It is God's plan for all of us to reach out in love. The tendencies which oppose that plan are isolation, criticism, lack of forgiveness and hatred.

Maria advises, "Be careful. Hate destroys the soul." Tanya says, "Think before you speak so you don't hurt people. That way you won't have bitter memories."

Sometimes people are afraid to love because they have been hurt or rejected in the past. Those closest to them should regularly reassure them: "I'm so glad you live with us." "You've al-

God's Plan

ways given me so much love." "I can tell how much you love your grandchildren." "You add so much to our supper table."
Sometimes love is blocked by unforgiveness or estrangement from a friend or family member. Do what you can to bring about reconciliation. If the other person is unwilling to be reconciled, your parent can still forgive, praying that God will continue to soften the hearts of everyone involved. As long as there is estrangement, there will be pain for all those involved.

Hope

God wants his children to have a lively hope founded on his love for them. This hope stands in clear contrast to depression, which finds no purpose in living any longer.
People whose health is failing often experience depression. They may say, "I don't understand why God has let me live so long. My life no longer has meaning or purpose."
I asked several hope-filled seniors how they would counsel someone who expressed this kind of depression.
Cora responded, "I can't imagine! Why in this wonderful world would anyone say that?"
Others were more sympathetic. Robbie advised, "When someone is depressed, try to find the reason. The death of a spouse, worries about money, feeling confined and unable to get out—all can make a person sad. Maybe she needs to talk about someone close who has died. Maybe she needs help with finances or medical problems that seem overwhelming. Maybe she just needs a friend to be there for her day after day."
Others would remind the depressed person, "God always has a purpose; keep praying to understand it." "God calls us home when our work on earth is done. There must be a reason he's let us live this long!"
A practical suggestion is to reach out to someone else. "There's always somebody worse off than you are," says Muriel. "Try to cheer up someone else."
In some cases, depression or other uncharacteristic reactions may signal a temptation from Satan. He is God's enemy,

21

and of course it angers him to see people draw closer to God in any way.

Nan gives an example. "One day my mother wasn't acting like herself. She was very depressed and kept saying, 'I wish I were dead. I'm no use to anyone; I'm just a burden.' Nothing I said to the contrary seemed to have any effect on her. She kept me at arm's length.

"I began to pray silently, asking Jesus to deliver her from whatever was oppressing her. Within five minutes, there was a dramatic change. She began chatting about ordinary details in her life, the self-accusation vanished, and she patted my shoulder affectionately on her way by."

In Psalm 31, the psalmist talks about being freed from the enemy's snare. Sometimes decisive action may be necessary to remove the snare, as with Nan's mother. At other times, freeing a parent requires much more patience and painstaking labor. I try to surround my mother-in-law with love, speak the truth to her often ("God loves you and created you for a purpose, I love you. . . ."), and cleanse my own heart of resentment and impatience. Little by little, she becomes free of "the grip of the enemy," as the psalmist puts it.

Perseverance

As parent and child strive together for holiness, you will quickly discover it is a long-term project. What God asks is not instant perfection but swift repentance as soon as our sinfulness is exposed.

Dolores advises, "Be patient with yourself and your mother. Ambivalence and resentment inevitably creep in. I talk to the Lord about it and go on, rather than becoming paralyzed with guilt at not being the perfect daughter or caregiver.

"No matter how hard we both try, we're going to make mistakes. We just have to admit them, quickly seek and give forgiveness. When attitudes, actions and words slip out that are thoughtless or even mean, apologize quickly and get on with loving. Keep asking for God's help and doing the best you can."

In the fourth chapter we will talk more about the attitudes

God's Plan

children should have toward their aging parents. Here let me simply point out that God calls children to grow in the same areas as their parents: believing, trusting, being grateful, loving, learning, hoping, repenting and forgiving.

Several children who have cared for parents in their homes summarize the growth that they themselves have experienced through this service.

Roger says, "Our family learned how to work out differences between generations. Personally, I became more eager to serve and developed abilities I never dreamed of. Looking back, I can see God's hand in everything, his loving care and at times his miraculous intervention."

Trish asks, "What have I learned from having Mother live with me? I have seen the world through the eyes of an 80-year-old. I have discovered many of my own inadequacies and my strengths. You do what you have to do when you have to do it! We have been angry with each other. We have climbed mountains of forgiveness. We have learned there is a time to speak and a time to keep silent."

Dolores reflects on friendships with several older women, including her mother. "My greatest gift to them was just consistently being there for them, injecting some novelty into their lives. Their gift to me was to help me grow in patience, persistence and awareness of how special and different each of us is, and how God loves us all. Each woman was also a fascinating door back into history."

She continues, "Mom and I always had very different interests and temperaments. My struggle to grow into independent adulthood caused conflict between us. When I moved back home to take care of her as she was dying, some of these issues reemerged. As before, I found it difficult to maintain my adult identity while I was living at home.

"With time and effort, we grew in respect for one another. We became friends as well as mother and daughter. I learned to understand and value the differences in our personalities and temperaments, instead of letting them be a source of conflict.

"God helped me overcome selfishness so I could offer help joyfully, with a sense of humor. I learned that my life and my time were not my own, and that this was right for the specific situation I was in.

"As my acceptance grew, commitment and duty turned into love and grace. It was a miracle! God renewed 'a steadfast spirit' (Ps. 51:12) within me, changing what I couldn't seem to change."

Chapter Three

Practical Advice In Caring for Parents

Medical Matters

Finding the right personal physician makes all the difference in the world. Even if specialists do get involved, your aging parent needs a primary physician who can coordinate care in a way that pays attention to her as a person. One family ran into major problems because two different physicians were prescribing medications. One would put the patient on a medication, she would tell the other she didn't know why she was taking it and he would take her off it! Pharmacists are pretty good at checking interactions among different drugs, but this is better done by the primary physician.

Denise, whose mother suffered from mental as well as physical illness, had a lot of bad experiences before she found the right doctor. "I questioned one doctor about the medications Mom was taking, so I could understand what was going on. I thought she was having some bad side-effects. I tried to approach it calmly, but the physician reacted very defensively. He said, 'This is what I charge, this is the care I give, I know what I'm doing, and if you don't trust me your mother can just find another physician.'

"After this experience, I decided to change doctors. Before

You and Your Aging Parent

our first appointment, I took careful notes on what I had noticed about my mother's behavior. When I began reading them to the new physician, he was puzzled. Why did I feel I had to prove anything to him? 'She's your mother,' he said. 'Of course you know what you're talking about. Here's what I recommend. Let's try the medication at this dosage and see how it works. Please check back with me in three days and let me know what you think.'

"I couldn't believe the difference! Fortunately, mother also felt comfortable with the second doctor; he listened to her and respected her a great deal."

Many factors go into choosing a physician. A convenient location is probably not the most important. Sarah confesses, "I took her to the dentist across the street from her nursing home because that was convenient for me, not because it was good for her. He did a perfunctory cleaning of her teeth and ignored her discomfort. When I finally took her to the best dentist I could find, we learned that several teeth needed crowns. It was an ordeal for her, but he worked patiently to put them on. She only had those crowns for a year before she died, but she was so proud of them! They made it so much easier for her to eat, and it was well worth the time and expense!"

Here are some questions to guide your choice.

Do health-care professionals and friends who have consulted this doctor respect his skill? When a doctor is very competent but has no bedside manner, the choice is much more difficult. If the patient is forewarned of this, she may be able to handle it without feeling he is uncaring or has something against her.

Is the doctor comfortable working with older people? Sometimes a younger M.D. may actually be more knowledgeable about geriatrics, but he has to be able to relate to the patient, not just the caregiver. Sarah had the following experience with a specialist. "After a series of strokes, my mother was confined to a wheelchair and unable to speak. That didn't mean she had no feelings or preferences about things! It used to annoy me so much when a doctor would walk right by my mother and start talking to me! I learned to stop him and say, 'Doctor, I'd like you to meet my mother, Estelle. Mom, this is Dr. So-and-so. He's here to find out why your back is hurting

Practical Advice

so much.' That simple introduction completely changed how one specialist related to her!"

Will the doctor take the patient's complaints seriously and investigate them thoroughly without ordering a lot of unnecessary tests? Some doctors dismiss the real difficulties of older people as hypochondria or the inevitable effects of old age. If a younger person came in with the same symptoms, they'd be much more aggressive in getting to the root of the problem and finding a solution. The fact that someone is old doesn't mean she should have to suffer with a curable illness or endure pain that the proper medication or therapy could control. Just because a person will never again do cartwheels is no reason not to rehabilitate her after a stroke or hip fracture so she can dress herself and walk to the bathroom!

Doreen says, "After surgery, Mom was in so much pain she could barely move. The pain gradually subsided, but she had gotten into the habit of favoring the tender places and was afraid to move very much. Inactivity led to depression. Finally I asked her doctor if physical therapy might help. We learned some exercises she could even do lying in bed. Not only was she able to move better, but she regained her zest for living."

At the other extreme, some doctors may intervene to prolong the patient's life beyond the point where she would choose to prolong it. Is the doctor comfortable discussing questions like these with the patient and the family? Will he willingly carry out your mother's wishes?

How directive is the doctor? How much direction does your mother want? Will he tell her what to do, and will she do it? Many parents are distrustful of doctors, reluctant to consult them. They may let something go for a long time. Children who suspect this is the case may be forced to intervene.

Tina reports, "My dad wouldn't go to a doctor, even though his feet were giving him a lot of trouble. He was afraid he might wind up in the hospital. Instead, he tried home remedies, and his feet got worse and worse. When he came to visit us, I took one look at his purple, swollen feet and burst into tears. I took him to a foot doctor, but he thought it was probably heart or kidney trouble. When the infection didn't clear up in a few days, Dad did have to go to the hospital.

"He was very restless and impatient to leave the hospital. I could tell he was blaming me for putting him there and didn't believe for a minute that it was for his own good. I felt very bad about this, but a priest helped me understand that Dad was just taking out his frustration on me and I shouldn't take it personally.

"Dad only lived for a month after he left the hospital, but he lived with us and we grew much closer in that short time."

Those who are responsible for their parent's day-to-day care quickly learn what is normal for the older person and what may be a danger signal.

One time, my mother-in-law developed pneumonia rather quickly. At first it was "just a cold," so I didn't take it very seriously. I thought all I had to do was keep her supplied with tissues! However, the cold quickly moved down into her chest and she developed a persistent deep cough. She became dehydrated and had to be hospitalized.

The next time she got a cold, I acted more quickly. I ran a cool-mist vaporizer in her bedroom at night and made sure she took plenty of liquids, including juices and chicken broth. She also liked Gatorade-type drinks, which restore balance for old people just as they do for athletes. A little Vicks VapoRub under her nose and on her chest helped open nasal and bronchial passages. Like the children, she liked hot water with honey and lemon juice when her throat was sore.

I tried these home remedies, but I also tried to be alert for signs of more serious illness: dry skin and flushed face which might mean dehydration, croupy cough with some color to her sputum, difficulty drawing breath or rapid, shallow breathing. I was ready to take her to the doctor sooner, and not to be embarrassed if he said, "Her lungs are clear; she just has a cold." That would have been better than winding up in the hospital emergency room with the doctor telling us we should have come in sooner.

Even after consulting a doctor, older people may not be willing or able to follow through on his directions. Some distrust medication of any kind. When they start to feel better, they may discontinue a medicine without checking with the doctor. Other seniors are always reading about new treatments

Practical Advice

and may consult new doctors in order to get prescriptions for additional medicines, often without exploring their side effects or how they interact with medications they are already taking.

Do you know what medications your mom takes, over-the-counter as well as prescription? She should know what each one is for, how to take it and what side effects it can have. If she gets all her medicines from the same pharmacist, he or she can be alert to possible interactions among them.

Shirley says, "Mom stopped taking her medicine without even telling her doctor. We were lucky we found out about it. I just happened to ask whether she'd like one of those pill reminders to keep track of her medications. She said she didn't need one, since she was only taking one kind of medicine. That wasn't what I remembered. When I questioned her I discovered she'd discontinued one type of medicine because it was too expensive and didn't seem to be helping her.

"I insisted she schedule an appointment and tell her doctor what she'd done. If she hadn't, I would have considered calling him myself. Perhaps she had made a good decision, but it was dangerous to act without consulting her doctor."

Some older people may also be unwilling or unable to follow a doctor's orders involving changes in diet or life-style: to give up smoking, for example, or to lose weight or to eat properly to control diabetes or heart disease. The older a person is, the harder it is to change the way she has always done things.

You have a dilemma if you see your parents making harmful choices. When do you need to respect those choices, and when is it time to intervene?

Make sure your parents understand the consequences of their choices. What's likely to happen if she refuses to avoid sugar or salt, for example? Is this what she really wants? If she hears all the facts and still makes a life-threatening choice, this may indicate she is no longer fully capable of making rational decisions and should be in a more protected environment. Especially if it is a question of diet, unwillingness to change may be her way of saying that preparing meals has become overwhelming for her. On the other hand, she may decide that the possible benefits of losing weight or giving up smoking are too slight to justify going through the trauma involved.

Try to find out as much as you can about your parent's medical condition, without conveying distrust of either your parent or the doctor.

Legal and Financial Matters

It is prudent for an aging parent to inform at least one of her children about her assets, debts, insurance policies, will and other documents. Where does she keep records of such things?

If she owns her own home, is there a mortgage? Who holds it and on what terms? Where is the deed? What does she want done with the property when she dies or becomes incapacitated?

Is there a list of her valuables, perhaps in connection with her homeowner's insurance? Are there specific items she wants to go to certain individuals after she dies?

Has her will been updated recently? Where is it? Who is her attorney? Her executor?

What insurance does she carry, and who needs to be notified in case of illness, accident, theft, death or another event affecting insurance?

Where are her bank accounts and other investments? What will happen to these when she dies? Does she have an accountant or financial adviser familiar with these matters?

What regular sources of income does she have, such as Social Security, pensions and interest on investments? What will happen to these when she dies? Who needs to be notified if she dies?

Have any arrangements been made with a funeral home? Does she own a cemetery plot? (One son was surprised to find that his mother had purchased lots for herself in seven different cemeteries!) What kind of wake and funeral does she want?

Does she have a living will or other document spelling out her decisions about life-prolonging procedures? If feasible, discuss medical options and what she thinks about steps doctors or hospitals might propose to make her comfortable, give time for the family to be with her or keep her alive indefinitely.

Someone should have durable power of attorney, including

Practical Advice

power of attorney for medical decisions, so that things do not grind to a halt if she becomes incapacitated.

Medical insurance can be bewildering. It is important to keep careful records of all bills, Medicare payments and payments from other insurers. Most older people have at least one supplemental insurance policy in addition to Medicare. Those who have exhausted their financial resources qualify for Medicaid.

Some doctors and hospitals accept assignment. This means they will be satisfied with whatever payment Medicare determines as fair for a specific service or procedure, even though their original bill was for a higher amount. This doesn't mean that Medicare pays the entire amount; patients are usually responsible for a copayment, often 20 percent of the adjusted amount. Most doctors' offices will file the insurance claim with Medicare; all they need is a copy of the patient's Medicare card. Some will file the supplemental insurance claim, but this cannot be done until Medicare sends notification about the approved total and how much it is paying. After payment has been received from Medicare and any supplementary insurer, the patient is responsible for the rest of the bill. To complicate matters further, some insurance companies pay the doctor directly, others want the patient to pay and will then reimburse her.

To keep all this straight, it is essential to have a good filing system. Bills should be arranged by date of service, with all correspondence (notices from Medicare and insurance companies, for example) attached to the original bill. Find out exactly what procedure is followed by each doctor's office and each insurer. You can do your parent a great service by helping her set up such a filing system or make sense of medical insurance mail which has already arrived.

Your parent may need help keeping track of debts, statements and invoices. If she is beginning to lose her memory, she may forget where she put her money, her bills or both. This may be a sign that she needs a different living situation and/or needs someone to begin exercising power of attorney for her. It may also be necessary to take away her credit cards, after discussing this with her. Such measures should not be taken

31

lightly; they directly affect a person's treasured independence. However, it's important to protect her from excessive debt or finance charges.

Miscellaneous Tips and Observations

In the course of our lives, most of us accumulate a great many possessions. Some are treasures laden with memories, but others may be broken, useless or even dangerous. One wise couple says, "We're trying to cut down the clutter by getting rid of six things in every closet and drawer every year. We really don't need all these things, and we don't want our children to have to sort through them after we're gone."

How do older people spend their time? One delightful lady says, "Everyone of every age deserves to have fun, something to look forward to!"

I have an older friend who loves to go to the local shopping mall. She doesn't buy anything, she just sits on a bench and talks to people, then goes home when she's tired. She says it's like therapy, except that it doesn't cost anything!

Don't assume your parents will want to do everything that interests you, but don't exclude them without asking. For example, we assumed Mom would have no interest in attending a minor league baseball game, but at the last minute she begged to come along and wound up having a wonderful time.

Beth shares about her mother: "A grandchild's wedding or the birth or baptism of a baby are so important to my mother. For months, she frets about what she's going to wear, how her hair will look, how she will get there, whether she'll tremble too much and embarrass herself, whether she'll become exhausted and have to leave early. Sometimes I wonder if it's worth all the trouble, but when I see her face shining during the event, I know the answer.

"Planning for a special event energizes Mom and gives her something to look forward to. It gives her a reason to take care of herself, to eat well, to exercise, perhaps to get out and go shopping. At the event itself, she forgets herself and does all she can to make the occasion special for others; her love and en-

Practical Advice

thusiasm are infectious. She makes contact with people she hasn't seen for a long time. That means a lot to her and to them.

"There can be a letdown after the event, but she has precious memories to share with those around her. Looking at the pictures, the program and other souvenirs is a joyous occupation, and I have sometimes enlisted her help in putting together a photo album or scrapbook. Knowing that she was able to attend the event also gives her courage that she can handle the next expedition or challenge."

Learn to slow down in communicating with your parents. The more rapidly someone speaks, the more difficult it is for an older person to assimilate the information and make an appropriate response.

Joy recounts, "I observed this while Dad was in the hospital. A young surgeon bounced into the room and began rattling off his analysis of Dad's condition. He had a lot to say about how long it would take for Dad to recover and what he should do in the meantime. Dad nodded his head, but I could tell he wasn't taking in a quarter of what the doctor said; it just came too fast!

"Dad isn't senile, but he doesn't think as fast as he used to. It takes longer for him to process what's said to him. I make a conscious effort to speak more slowly and to pause between thoughts, especially when I'm presenting a series of steps or ideas. I also ask Dad for feedback to make sure he's understood. When others speak too fast, I interrupt when I can. 'Whoa, Doc,' I'll say, 'could you run that by us a little slower? What do those test results mean again?' "

CHAPTER FOUR

Growth in Understanding

We have discussed decisions about practical matters such as medical care, finances and schedule. In the next chapter we will consider another major practical decision, where your parents should make their home. In this chapter, we turn to matters of wisdom and understanding rather than knowledge and common sense. How can you deal with your own feelings and experiences as you try to care for your aging parents? What obstacles must be overcome? What gifts and graces should you pray for and cultivate so you can be a better caregiver?

Compassion

What every caregiver needs most of all is compassion.

Dolores puts it well. "I try to be patient with Mom, to understand what it's like to walk in her slippers, not only to understand but to sympathize. I'm intelligent enough to understand most of the time, but compassion doesn't come so easily. When I'm compassionate, I know God is answering my prayers.

"I ask myself how I would feel if I couldn't hear well and people were impatient with me or allowed the conversation to pass me by rather than making an extra effort to include me.

"How would I feel if I couldn't go anywhere unless someone took me, especially if others were impatient and communicated, even indirectly, what an inconvenience it was?

35

"How would I feel if my hands shook so much that I often spilled drinks and continued shaking so I couldn't even regain my dignity by helping to clean up?

"How would I feel if I was helplessly incontinent and couldn't clean myself up?

"The list goes on and on. I try to be patient and understanding as I apply the Golden Rule. How, indeed, would I feel, and how would I want to be treated?"

Some parents are very difficult to love. Melanie discovered some ways to improve her relationship with her father. "My father is very difficult to get along with. He's full of life and has a wonderful sense of humor, but he's impatient and demanding. It's impossible to please him.

"I used to explode almost every time we visited him, but then I began to look for reasons for his behavior. Dad had been an only child in a family that had to scrape to survive; he didn't learn a lot of social skills there. I discovered something else that helped me a lot. When Dad seemed extra-irritable, there was usually a reason: an old friend had died, he was experiencing a new pain, he was having trouble sleeping because of a new medication. . . . In other words, he gave others the hardest time when he himself was having a hard time.

"I became a detective, trying to find out what was upsetting him. Sometimes I could do something to make things better for him, sometimes I couldn't, but I was more peaceful when I understood what was going on and gave him some emotional support. I wanted him to know I loved him unconditionally, however he happened to be feeling or behaving."

If your parent is grieving or apprehensive, she needs extra assurances of your love. No one can replace her husband, but it helps if you supply plenty of hugs and affectionate touches, extra phone calls, notes and visits, and the words "I love you" in many forms.

Humility

Even adult children have a great deal to learn from their parents. As teenagers, most of us were too self-absorbed to do

Growth in Understanding

this, but as we grow older we usually grow in appreciation for our parents' wisdom.

Ruth gives one example, but there are countless others. "I'm still learning charity from my mother's words and example. I've never heard her say a bad word about anyone. If I begin to complain about a co-worker, she'll stop me short. 'Now, that's not charitable,' she says. That ends the matter!"

One specific thing you should try to learn is how your parents want to be cared for. Some parents will be able to put this into words if asked specific questions. Otherwise, you'll have to watch carefully to find out what's helpful and pleasing. What kind of music does Mom like? What scents does she like and what smells make her turn up her nose? Which ways of touching annoy her and which soothe her?

Philippians 2:3-4 urges Christians to defer to one another, to "think humbly of others as superior to [yourselves], each of you looking to others' interests rather than to [your] own." Try to care for your mother the way she wants to be cared for, rather than the way you prefer. For example, perhaps you are a very spontaneous person but your mother likes things more scheduled and orderly. Perhaps she wants to be able to count on having her bath and her meals at the same time each day. If you provide this basic structure, she'll be more receptive to your spontaneous expressions of love.

Fran gives another example. "Small details are very important to Mother. Even though she stays home most of the time, she really wants her shoes polished and her makeup carefully applied.

"My sister helped me understand this. She reminded me how meticulous Mother used to be about our appearance when we were growing up. So now I try to pay attention to her preferences, to replace shoelaces before they become frayed, to take time with her grooming, to keep her things in good order. If it matters to her, it matters! She's much happier when I anticipate her desires in this area rather than waiting until she becomes irritated."

A word of caution is in order here. While most parents are extremely reluctant to be a burden in any way, some do make unreasonable demands. Such a parent may insist that you and no one else cater to all her whims. She may make you feel guilty when you don't do what she wants. She may have a temper tantrum or act depressed, as if she has no reason to go on living if you can't do the tiniest thing for her. She may interfere with decisions that should rightfully be made by you and your husband for the good of your marriage and family. If you find yourself giving in to unreasonable demands, perhaps you've never really cut the apron strings. This isn't healthy for you or your mother.

However, you should never refuse to meet your mother's legitimate needs, however she expresses them. You can often bring her joy by anticipating her preferences as well as her needs. Try not to let selfish considerations and your own emotional reactions sway you from doing what is in her best interest.

Anita puts it succinctly. "You have to give her what she needs, not limit it to what you think you're able to give. This is a stretch!"

Building a Relationship

It takes time to build and maintain a good relationship with your parent or any older person.

A 92-year-old says, "Looking for a gift suggestion? Give an older person a gift of time! Invite her to attend a play, to tell you stories from her past, to listen to old songs or to enjoy a favorite dish you've prepared for her. This can work to everyone's advantage: younger people often need the attention an older person can give. The time and love you invest will last forever. You'll have no regrets. Each day is a gift from God, so share it with sisters and brothers in Christ."

I try to remember that Mom won't be around forever and I should take advantage of the time I have left, spending relaxed, quality time with her. I'm just beginning to realize that I, too, will be old someday.

Yes, I'm busy with many things, some that are important (helping a child decide where to apply for college), as well as some that are rather trivial. Mom doesn't make many demands on me, while the children and the housework call out for atten-

Growth in Understanding

tion. It's easy to overlook her need for companionship and understanding.

I try to set aside time just to be with her, to give her my whole attention rather than half-listening while my mind is occupied with something else. This doesn't have to be a great deal of time, but it needs to be high-quality time, and I shouldn't be fretting about when I can get back to more important work. "Wasting" time together is very important in building or strengthening a relationship. On my own I might never choose to watch a ballgame on television or to look through old photo albums. Since these activities are important to Mom, though, they are important. I love her by setting aside my preferences. Sometimes I even learn to enjoy things I didn't appreciate before!

The Lord is teaching me that it's not my time to use as I please, but his time to please him with.

Building a relationship can be hard work. Nell confesses, "I didn't know what to say to my father. I'd always been able to talk with Mom, but my relationship with Dad was more distant. I don't remember sharing any of the small or great events in my life with him.

"Then suddenly Mom was gone and Dad was gravely ill. He wanted his children with him, though he didn't need us to do any specific thing for him. I felt awkward just sitting there; I've always identified with Martha rather than Mary in the Gospel story. Yet I knew I was supposed to be there.

"It seemed artificial at first, but on my way to see Dad I planned what I'd talk about. I paid attention to the weather so I could describe it to him. I reviewed what I'd done since I last saw him. What could I share with him? Had the children done or said something amusing? Had there been a mix-up at work, or a happy coincidence? What was I working on and planning?

"I also began to ask myself what I wanted to learn from my father. What questions could I ask to help piece together the part of his life I hardly knew? How had he met Mom? What was his first job? What were his hopes for me before I was born? What practical advice could he give me? What really mattered to him? What were some of his favorite things? I began jotting down his answers, and I later discovered that there are blank 'grandparent books' to help organize a person's memories for the grandchildren.

"Gradually I became comfortable sitting silently with my father; we didn't need to be talking all the time. As he weakened, conversation became more of a strain for him. However, I often said, 'I love you,' 'I'm with you,' 'I appreciate you,' 'I'm thankful for you, and for this special time.' "

Another daughter worked at building a relationship with her father by telephone after her mother died. The first common interest she discovered was grocery coupons!

Again and again, children stress the importance of good communication. Claire talks affectionately about her relationship with her mother. "Mom and I are very straightforward with each other. If either of us has a problem, we get it out into the open right away and work it through. We feel free to correct each other, and we both take correction well, making the necessary changes, then moving on without holding a grudge. Neither of us is high-falutin' or pompous, and we laugh a lot together about our diminishing power to remember things."

Bobbie says, "I try to keep communication very open between us. Sometimes things just don't feel right or I sense a strain in the relationship. At times like this, I pray before talking with Mom. Sometimes I also ask her to pray about a specific area before we discuss it together. Listening to the Lord helps free both of us from getting set in our ways and helps us listen to each other better, too."

Prayer

Bobbie's comments bring us to another important point. We have so many resources available to us: medicines and medical knowledge, good books, the experience and support of friends. Wonderful as these things are, Christians have a more powerful tool we often neglect. Why is prayer so often our last resort instead of our first recourse?

Bobbie continues, "Often I know something is wrong but I don't know just what. Does my attitude need changing? Is Mom having a new medical problem? Am I trying to do too much? Are my expectations too high? Should I point out to her

Growth in Understanding

that a certain expression she uses sounds rude? Is something bothering or worrying her that she hasn't been able to talk about?

"Again and again, I've taken problems to the Lord in prayer, seeing no way out, and he's given me light about what to do or how I need to change, followed by the grace to follow through on what he's shown me.

"It's also important for me to pray for Mom: that her needs will be met and that she'll be free from sickness, anxiety, depression or whatever is bothering her."

Try to make sure your parents' spiritual needs are met. If they've moved, they've probably lost contact with their familiar pastor and church community. Perhaps you attend a church in a different denomination. You may not be very familiar with your parents' spiritual needs or religious habits. To compound the problem, if your parents have always regarded religion as a private matter, they may find it difficult to communicate or even to recognize their spiritual needs.

Nevertheless, these needs are basic. You may have to do some legwork before you find a church and a pastor who can relate well to your parents, but making this connection is vital.

Mismatched Expectations

Conflicts arise when you and your parent expect different things. This can cause the two of you to work at cross-purposes and to resent what seems like pushing or resisting. Forthright communication can resolve such differences, but first someone has to recognize what is going on!

Briege says, "I couldn't understand why my efforts to help Mom with her physical therapy caused so many tears. Finally I realized the two of us had very different goals. I wanted Mom to regain mobility after her surgery. All she wanted was to be free of pain.

"Once we got this out in the open, I was able to accept her goal and give up my higher expectations. Knowing our goal, the therapist could tell us how much to exercise and how much discomfort to tolerate."

Edna found herself in a different situation when her grandmother stayed with her temporarily after a stroke. Grandma wanted to be able to function well enough to move back into her own home. However, the therapy necessary to achieve this goal was so difficult it was easy to lose sight of the objective. Then Grandma would lash out at Edna for being so hard on her. Edna often took the criticism personally and backed down from her demands. Because they never talked honestly and clearly about this, their relationship became strained and neither accomplished what she really wanted. The therapy hurt more than Grandma liked, yet didn't accomplish their shared goal of making her self-sufficient. Each woman tried to do her best, but there was a lot of guilt and blame on both sides.

I have a similar dilemma. How can I get Mom to do what I feel she needs to do? It's so frustrating when she refuses to do things that would improve her life immeasurably, solving difficulties she herself recognizes. For example, she complains about not being able to hear, but refuses to get a hearing aid. What can I do? Every once in a while I suggest again that she get a hearing aid, and at times she seems more open to the idea. If she ever agrees to this, I can help her to follow through on her decision, but that decision must be hers, not mine!

When should I nudge Mom forward and when should I just let her be? Sometimes I try to encourage her to push herself just a little more, but she thinks I'm finding fault. That's not at all what I want or mean to do. If she perceives it that way, I ask forgiveness and we go on from there.

One kind of mismatched expectation is very common. Phyllis gives a good example of this. "Sometimes I try to solve Mom's problems when all she wants is someone to listen to her! This became clear to me one day when she began complaining about meals in the retirement center. I asked what she'd had for lunch that day. Then I said it sounded more nutritious than what I'd served my children. She snapped, 'Whose side are you on, anyway?'

"That made me realize I should close my mouth and really listen to what she was saying, to try to understand and sympathize. Then sometimes we could move beyond that. Since then, I try to ask a leading question before I offer advice, for example, 'Would you like to hear what I'd do if I were in your

Growth in Understanding

situation?' That gives her an opportunity to say yes or no, and I respect her answer. Before jumping in with advice, I try to find out what she wants from me. Sometimes it's advice, but more often it's just sympathy and unconditional acceptance."

Personality Differences

In any close relationship, there are bound to be disagreements. Each person and each generation has a different set of experiences and of things they take for granted. There is no point in trying to argue about these. Technically, you may win an argument, but only because age has dulled your parent's debating ability; you will not persuade her.

Personality differences can also cause tension. This may be more striking if you are suddenly spending more time together after being separated for a number of years. In those years, each of you has grown and changed through experiences the other knows nothing about. You may also have different memories of the last time you lived together (perhaps it was when you were a child). Similarities in personality can be even more irritating than differences.

Doreen, whose mother now lives with her, says, "My mother and I are so different! Sometimes she'll shake her head and say, 'You're not the daughter I raised!' In many ways, she's right. I left home as a teenager and never really returned, which means many people and events have influenced me besides my parents.

"When Mom says something like this, it's like a red flag. I try to understand what she's saying before I respond. Did she misunderstand what I just said or did, interpreting it on the basis of some experience I don't share? If we really do disagree, do we need to come to an agreement, or can we respectfully agree to disagree? I sometimes find I'm clinging to an opinion simply to be different; changing it wouldn't harm my integrity at all.

"As we've explored such questions, we've found we have more in common than we thought. Now that I'm an adult, I'm beginning to appreciate what a neat person my mother is. We've also discovered rich memories from my childhood, shared experiences I hardly noticed as a child but which we can now recall with joy."

Bea adds, "Although our different personalities grate on each other, I've learned that I have a choice in this. These differences can be a constant source of irritation, rubbing me the wrong way all the time, or they can have the effect of sand in an oyster, creating a pearl, giving me opportunities to grow in holiness and to prepare my mother for heaven.

"What makes the difference? It helps when we can talk openly, and ask and receive forgiveness. However, we can't always do this. Then I find great comfort and insight in prayer and in my husband's wise advice. He keeps reminding me that my personal worth comes from my heavenly Father, not from what my mother thinks of me. He also urges me to set aside my preferences and treasure my mother as she is, just as I would gladly serve Christ if he were a guest in our home. I wouldn't expect him to share all my likes and dislikes, but I would do my best to make him comfortable by providing what he liked. So I try to overlook my mother's irritating behavior and serve her willingly."

Jealousy

Jealousy is often a hidden factor, especially between mother-in-law and daughter-in-law. On the conscious level, every mother wants what is best for her son, but if that takes him away from her the adjustment can be very difficult.

Shanna tells her story. In her mother-in-law's case, intense jealousy was a sign of mental illness. This is not typical. However, similar factors are often at work in more normal relationships as well.

"My mother-in-law is very jealous of me. When I first met her, she was warm and welcoming. As Greg and I moved closer to engagement, though, she became more ambivalent. I don't think she has ever recognized her own resentment and jealousy, but it has been a big factor in our relationship.

"Greg is her youngest son and he lived with her until we were married. Since his father had died 10 years earlier, in many ways Greg took his place. Mom assumed he would al-

Growth in Understanding

ways be there to care for her. Suddenly I intruded on that arrangement! Even though I tried to assure her that we both loved her and would continue to take care of her, she felt threatened. Our wedding precipitated a nervous breakdown. Eventually she returned home with medication and ongoing therapy, but her suspicion and resentment have remained beneath the surface and occasionally reemerge.

"Although her case is extreme, I don't think jealousy between mother-in-law and daughter-in-law is that uncommon. Now I understand it from the other side. Although my son is only seven, I can imagine myself being quite possessive of him as an adult. I love him so dearly that I know no woman can ever take care of him as he deserves!

"After being in this situation, I can only hope and pray that I will be a good mother-in-law when my turn comes, moving out of the way so my son can get on with God's plan for his life."

In a less extreme case, Doug and Rose found practical ways to deal with his mother's jealousy. After she moved in with them, her jealousy occasionally surfaced through sharp words or negative humor about her daughter-in-law. Rose says, "When this happened, my husband defended me, making it clear that he stood behind my decisions. His mother's love for him was unconditional, while she seemed to love me more for what I did for her. This gave him the freedom to deal with her when she spoke inappropriately to me or about me."

Role Reversal

As your parents decline physically, they may become dependent on you for basic care. This reverses the earlier pattern of parents caring for their dependent children. The shift in roles can be hard on everyone.

Briege recounts her experience. "Since infancy, this woman has taken care of me. How strange it seems that now I am caring for her: preparing her meals, tucking her into bed, keeping track of her schedule. The change is difficult for both of us!

"Once Mom said to an acquaintance, 'She's my mother now!' That made me very uncomfortable. I said, 'I have five children, but I only have one mother. Even though I care for some of your physical needs, I will always love and respect you as my mother.'

"I try to treat Mom with great respect. Even if I'm doing for her what I might do for a child, I always speak to her as an adult. I let her handle as many decisions as possible. I try to care for her according to her preferences rather than acting like I know what's best for her."

It's hard to maintain an adult-to-adult relationship. Sometimes the daughter is treating the parent as a child; at other times the parent continues to mother her daughter as if she weren't grown up. Sometimes, though, the only problem is in the way the daughter perceives things.

Briege continues, "I resented being treated like a child! Every time I dressed up in hose and put on my hat and coat, she'd ask, 'Where are you going? Are you dressed warmly enough? What time will you be back?' I bristled like a rebellious teenager who didn't want to be told what to do. I felt like saying, 'Mother, I'm 50 years old! Can't I go out without being interrogated?'

"My husband cut through all this for me. When I told him what happened, he asked sensibly, 'Why don't you just tell her where you're going?' So now I let her know where I'm going and when I expect to be back, and the problem has vanished!"

Dolores puts the problem in perspective. "It's hard to relate to my mother respectfully when I have to take care of her like a child. We both try to remember that God is Father to both of us. Before him, we are an elder and a younger sister with different abilities and limitations but always related in love."

Past Hurts

Unresolved hurts from the past can make it difficult for you to care for your parent, or for her to accept care from you.

Tina shares an experience of forgiving her parents that was very important for her. "My mother was a little older than my friends' mothers, and I thought she was terribly strict and old-fashioned. Now that I'm a parent myself, I begin to see how wise she was!

"One night, I heard a minister speak about forgiveness

Growth in Understanding

within families, and the message touched my heart. I went right home and called my parents. First I asked my mother to forgive me for all I had done, and she did; then I told her I had nothing against her anymore. I did the same with my dad.

"Things didn't change overnight. In fact, I remember having a fight with my mother the next time I went home! However, it was a new beginning, and I can't remember any fights after that."

Marilyn shares another story about forgiveness.

"At one point, I was having a hard time taking care of Mom. I was recuperating from surgery myself, and it was a physical strain to visit her every day and attend to her needs. I became frustrated, even angry that she needed me so much. When I prayed about it, God showed me that I was still angry about something that had happened during my adolescence. At that time I had felt my mother let me down by being too busy to listen to me.

"I was afraid to bring it up. It had happened so long ago, I thought my mother probably didn't even remember it! Then one day she confessed to me that she had always regretted not spending more time with me during those early teen years. She knew she couldn't make up for that lost time directly, but afterward she had tried to listen to young people who needed someone to talk with, like teenagers in her neighborhood. Many had, in fact, sought her out when they were troubled.

"I told her I forgave her. I was so proud of her for putting her repentance to such positive use!"

What if the wrongdoing was more serious and your parents have never accepted responsibility for it? What if they neglected or even abused you? Can you still forgive, even if they don't understand the meaning of forgiveness?

We are all God's debtors. If you realize you don't love your parent as God wants you to, you know yourself well; you are humble enough to take advantage of God's abundant mercy. Only by his grace can you forgive your parent in the unconditional way which will free both of you to give and receive the love of practical day-to-day care.

The decision to care for your parent should be based not on how you feel but on what is right and good for that parent.

Usually, doing the loving thing eventually generates loving feelings, but God's love can touch both of you even if loving feelings are faint and rare.

Josie says, "I can't talk to my mother about problems in our relationship. She'd react very emotionally with an exaggeration like, 'I guess I'm no _____ good. I should probably just drop dead!' There's no rational way to respond to a statement like that! She doesn't seem to be able to understand that a person can do or say something amiss without being 'no good' as a person.

"I've tried to deal with my anger and frustration about growing up in a critical, unaffectionate family by praying about it, asking the Lord to help me forgive my mother and to do the right thing for her, even though we can never resolve differences face to face or express affection very directly. This has helped me a lot."

Laura, whose father died recently, says, "I used to ask why I should have to take care of my dad. He wasn't around much during my childhood. Even when he was there, he never showed me any affection. I behaved because I was afraid he'd whip me, not because I wanted to please him.

"I know my father grew up in a neglectful, abusive situation. He protected himself by keeping others at an emotional distance. I still felt empty, but understanding his background helped me give up my anger, bitterness and harsh judgment.

"We took him into our home after a lot of prayer because we felt it was the right thing to do. Sometimes taking care of him was more an act of my will than something I felt like doing. I prayed that God would change my heart as I did loving things for him. I couldn't force him to be affectionate; I could only treat him with respect and tenderness. Sometimes he teased me about my TLC. Reading between the lines, I could tell he really appreciated what I did for him.

"Prayer and Christian teaching helped me a lot. I knew the Lord expected me to honor my parents. When I struggled with negative feelings and with the urge to abandon my duty, I prayed — sometimes pretty frank prayers — and God helped me to persevere.

"It also helped to talk with an older Christian woman. She

Growth in Understanding

never pressured me but patiently reminded me of what God wanted. She encouraged me to keep on.

"After my father died, I felt abandoned. A Christian friend urged me not to concentrate on how much Dad did or did not love me but to concentrate on how the Lord, my true Father, does love me."

Shanna tells how she brought her feelings to the Lord and how he intervened to set things right between her and her mother-in-law.

"Because of my mother-in-law's mental illness, our young family moved in with her. As we had hoped, this helped stabilize her emotionally. During our time there, she worked full-time and needed no psychological counseling.

"However, the move was hard on me. Knowing how tired she was from working all day, I chose to do all the cleaning, shopping and meal preparation. To please her, I even cooked two different meals some nights. Although I tried to do all this with a servant's heart, I often felt like a doormat. Never, during our six months in Mom's home, did I hear her say, 'Thank you.'

"The seed of resentment began to grow inside me. I cried, I prayed, I talked with Mom, with my husband, with a close friend, but this choking plant continued to grow.

"We finally decided that the strain of the living situation was too hard on our young family and that we needed a place of our own. Meanwhile Mom had developed physical problems that made professional medical care necessary. Reluctantly, we moved her into a nursing home.

"As her illness progressed, she became unable to speak and could only communicate by writing. One day she scrawled a request for me to come and cut her hair.

"I came into her room on Friday, shears in hand, and helped her to a chair where she sat, head hanging down. It took every ounce of her energy to hold herself in the chair. Despite her valiant cooperation, I couldn't make her hair fall the way I needed to get the cut right. Somehow I finished the job and got her back into bed. Objectively, it was a terrible haircut, but she felt better and I was so grateful I had been able to serve her in this way.

"Once back in bed, she motioned for her writing tablet.

Summoning every bit of energy, she managed to etch two words: 'Thank you.' I could tell by her eyes and her faint smile that she was not just showing appreciation for the haircut but for all the little things I had done for her over the past few years. I hugged her tight and told her I loved her.

"As I walked the few blocks home, I felt lighter. Finally I was free to love my mother-in-law without bitterness. In two short words, God had answered all my prayers.

"Mom was admitted to the hospital the next day and died on Sunday. She was buried in her favorite peach dress with the awful haircut that had been the occasion of our healing."

CHAPTER FIVE

Where Should They Live?

One of the most perplexing questions which aging parents and their children face is whether the parents should move. The question may arise because of retirement, the death of a spouse, a brush with crime in the neighborhood, an injury or illness, or a gradual decline in the parents' ability to care for themselves.

Options range from remaining in their own house to moving into a nursing home. There are also many home-care arrangements as well as a variety of retirement centers.

There is no magic formula for calculating whether or when it would be wise to move. However, changes and crises such as those mentioned above are natural times for reflecting on short- and long-term goals. A word of caution: Emotions run high during a crisis. Be sure you consider what will be best in the long run as well as what will solve the immediate problem.

It is usually easiest and most comforting to remain as long as possible in the family home where everything and everyone is familiar. Sometimes moving is a positive choice motivated by a desire to be closer to children and grandchildren, to live in a warmer climate or to have things like yardwork and household repairs done by someone else.

Unfortunately, negative reasons can also be very important. Mom may not want to move, but it becomes clear that she can no longer manage on her own. Ideally, you and your mother arrive at this realization at the same time and can work together toward a solution. In practice, it can be almost impossible to reach a decision that satisfies everyone concerned. Mom may feel it's time for a change before it occurs to you. More commonly, you become concerned for her well-being long before she recognizes or admits this need.

Who Decides?

Ordinarily, the final decision should be the parent's. There are obvious exceptions. Sufferers from Alzheimer's, for instance, cannot consistently care for themselves. A fractured hip or a condition requiring oxygen therapy may also make a different arrangement necessary, at least temporarily.

However, most parents are quite capable of deciding where and how they want to live. Children should try to understand these choices even though they may not agree with them.

Ideally, all those concerned in the decision — parents and all their children — should sit down together to make it. Even if such a meeting is not feasible, consultation should be extensive. People need to understand the realities of one another's lives, their expectations, their feelings and which options each considers acceptable and unacceptable.

Sometimes parents make firm decisions based on their own experience. If your mother cared for your elderly grandmother in her home, she may expect you to do the same for her — or she may decide she'll never burden you in that way! If her experience was a happy one, it may seem very natural to follow the same model. If, on the other hand, everyone expected her to take care of her mother and no one lifted a finger to help her do this, deep resentment may make it impossible for her to accept help from you, however willing you may be.

What can you do if Mom feels this way? Go ahead and offer to have her move in with you. Try to explain why you think this would work. Even if she refuses, your mother should know that the offer remains open. Repeat it gently from time to time. Try not to blame your mother for choosing something different from what you want for her. Help your mother make sure her basic needs are met, whether that means hiring someone to do burdensome tasks, or moving into a condominium, a retirement center or a nursing home.

Stepping in when a parent no longer has the mental capacity to make her own decisions can be wrenching for both parties. It is hard for children to admit that the parent who cared for them is no longer capable of caring for herself. On the other hand, the parent may think she's coping well, but her children are sure that it's dangerous for her to be on her own any longer.

Here is how one family handled this decision.

"Mom just couldn't take care of her home any longer. She couldn't rake leaves and shovel snow, haul laundry up from the basement and do the thorough spring cleaning that meant so much to her. For a while, her children who lived nearby pitched in to help her, and she hired people to do heavier work, but then other problems began to surface. When her doctor made a tentative diagnosis of Alzheimer's, we knew that Mom would need more help before long.

"As she became more forgetful, we began to worry about her safety. She didn't always remember to take her medicine. Sometimes she couldn't recall if she had eaten. She occasionally ruined a pan by leaving a stove burner on. Finally, one night, she got up to use the bathroom and fell down the stairs. She crawled back up and lay there until morning. She could have telephoned for help, but she didn't want to disturb anyone in the middle of the night!

"We tried having people check on her regularly, either friends or professionals who could cook a meal or help her bathe. She resisted this kind of help and there were too many hours between checks anyway. We wanted to find a place where someone could be with her round the clock.

"We noticed, too, that as she became more confused she didn't want to leave the house. Being alone so much made her depressed, and she had an even harder time taking care of herself.

"How could we persuade her to move? Her situation had changed so gradually, she didn't see the need clearly. She had elaborate strategies for making sure things were under control. She recorded everything she did on scraps of paper she kept on dressers, tabletops and every surface in the house.

"My siblings and I wanted to watch her more closely and agree on some options before we talked with Mom about changing anything. We gathered for a long weekend together. During that time we shared a lot of precious memories, our assessment of Mom's current needs, our thoughts and feelings about the future.

"My sister Janie had always assumed she'd care for Mom in her old age but realized she was not in a position to do that now. Her husband and Mom don't get along at all; there was constant tension when they were in the same room. Janie had young children and was trying to juggle their needs with the demands of a part-time job she'd taken to help pay the bills. They live a considerable distance from Mom, and during her last visit there Mom had trouble adjusting to the climate and the pace of life around Los Angeles.

"Before leaving for this family gathering, I had several long conversations with my husband and children. God has been very good to me! My parents loved and cared for me; I have a wonderful husband who earns enough so that I can be home with my children rather than working. I also have wise and supportive Christian friends.

"We knew having Mom move in wouldn't be easy for her or for us. Any change is difficult, especially a change which means giving up treasured independence. We had no romantic illusions about what it would mean to open our home to someone who was needy as well as gifted. Because I have friends who are doing this, I know that caring for an elderly parent, especially one whose health is failing, is hard work. I knew it would curtail my freedom and affect relationships within our family.

"Although our children loved their grandmother, they had mixed feelings about making space for her in our home and our lives. We didn't come to the decision democratically, but we did listen to their concerns and try to work out solutions to some of the problems we foresaw.

"Despite the challenges, when my husband and I looked at all our resources and then at my mother's need for a safe, loving environment, we decided to invite her to move in with us.

"We didn't want to force a change on Mom or present it to her in a way that would make her feel defensive or incompetent. We prayed that she would accept it, and then we all sat down to talk with her. The idea of a permanent move didn't appeal to her, but we got her to agree to come to our house for the winter. She was afraid she might fall on the ice if she remained at home, and it made sense to her to spend the winter with us.

"Once this decision was made, we worked together on the practical details. We set a moving date a month after our gathering to allow for preparations on both ends. Janie agreed to help her pack and travel to our home. My brother Steve said that, when Mom made a more permanent decision, he would go through the things in her house and decide what to sell, what to send her and what to distribute among the rest of us. We all made lists of things that were especially meaningful. Everyone agreed that Mom should pay us rent and that we would all divide any unusual medical or remodeling expenses. Everyone promised to keep in touch with her by mail and phone, to invite her to visit them, and to take turns staying with her so we could take family vacations.

"A neighbor kept Mom's walk shoveled and checked her house during those winter months; no one said anything about selling the house. However, it became increasingly evident to us that she couldn't return home. When we began talking about this with her in the spring, there were many tears and some anger, but she also grasped the reality of the situation. Once she took practical steps such as putting her house up for sale, she seemed more peaceful.

"It hasn't always gone smoothly, but having agreements with my brothers and sisters has helped a lot. They check in with me as well as with Mom, and we keep them informed about medical, financial and personal developments. I'm grateful for their involvement, and we all try to avoid blaming one another when things are less than perfect.

"This decision process and living it out have brought our family much closer together."

What Are the Options?

In deciding where an older person should live, one important consideration has to do with relationships.

Who are Mom's relatives and close friends? If she moves, can she stay in contact with these important people? Will any of them be involved in her care?

Some people are independent and able to form new relationships and maintain old ones. They can travel independently—either by driving or by using public transportation—to shop, exercise or participate in community groups based on service, companionship or common interests. These might include classes, a church guild, a bridge club, meals at a senior center or regular golf outings. These people enjoy being with others.

However, some seniors are loners, either by nature or because of a disability, shyness, fear or where they live. They may be unhappy where they are, yet they will find it difficult to adjust to new surroundings.

Arlene says, "My mother has chosen to remain in her own house even though she's lonely and scared. Ten years ago, when her mother was in an apartment complex for older folks, my mother often said she herself would like that. Now that my father is dead, however, she won't consider leaving her familiar house and all her possessions. This seems to be more important than having people nearby, though she has few friends and often complains of being lonely and bored.

"She says she would feel just as insecure in an apartment complex because tenants have keys made for relatives and 'Who knows who's coming in and out?' This makes me think that fear and loneliness have as much to do with the person as with the situation."

Remaining in Her Own Home

There are many practical and emotional reasons for a parent to stay put. She has probably paid off the mortgage. Living in her own home is therefore more economical than buying or renting a smaller place, even if it's more convenient. It's comforting to remain in a familiar home in a familiar town, with the support of friends and neighbors, church and clubs. She knows the local merchants and the layout of the local stores,

Where Should They Live?

where to find her favorite reading material at the library and what hours the bank is open. Her doctor, dentist, accountant and lawyer know her whole history.

If your mother lives by herself, here are some questions to help you assess whether she's managing all right.

Is her neighborhood safe? Does she feel secure in her home alone?

Does she seem fit, given her physical condition?

If she has a disability, is her home practical for her present situation? Can it be altered or remodeled to suit her needs?

Does she keep herself and her home reasonably clean?

Does she prepare nutritious meals for herself?

Does she take medications as directed and do they seem to be effective? Are you confident she will neither omit important medicine nor take an accidental overdose?

What are her sources of income and her predictable expenses? Do these balance out? Does she pay her bills on time?

Does she have proper insurance coverage?

You can help your parents assess needs for additional help and find the right people to meet those needs. This is discussed further in Chapter Seven. Even if all this is in place, it is wise to talk about future housing arrangements in case some major changes occur.

When it's time to make a move, what should that move be?

The major deciding factor is your parent's good, not your preference or convenience. The first question is not, "What can I do (or not do) for Mom?" The primary question is, "What's best for Mom?" Christians will also consider the question, "What is God's will?" Sometimes a deadlock among family members can be broken if they agree to give up their own preferences and seek God's will.

We will consider in turn the most common options, but there are other possibilities. An 84-year-old says, "I live with a single woman much younger than I. In fact, I knew her parents before they were married! This works very well for us. We have many common interests, but because of our age difference we don't expect or want to be involved with the same people or go to the same places all the time."

Moving into a Retirement Center

This decision will be made by the parent. If she asks for your advice, here are some factors to consider.

Every retirement center is different, but the basic idea is to provide on the same property a variety of levels of care. These usually include independent living (residents care for themselves but some meals, maintenance and housekeeping may be provided), custodial care (assistance with dressing, personal hygiene and taking medication), intermediate care (nursing care available at least 16 hours a day) and skilled nursing (complete health care, like a hospital without a surgical unit).

Once you have signed a contract, the institution often guarantees care until you die, although there are many different arrangements for financing this. Increasing longevity and unforeseen cost increases have caused 40 percent of these retirement centers to hover near bankruptcy. It is wise to investigate thoroughly before making a commitment to one.

A person should visit a retirement center several times before making a final decision. Some of these visits should be unannounced.

Get several copies of all brochures and contracts. Your parents should look them over carefully and show them to an attorney, an accountant and others they trust.

They should ask specific questions. If they don't understand the answers, they should ask again. Don't assume administrators understand your parents' situation and desires, or know more than they do. If what they hear sounds odd, it probably is!

Do some comparison shopping and talk with other families who have chosen this facility or others.

No one should be pressured into making a decision on the spot. (All this applies to selecting a nursing home, too.)

Some centers provide guest accommodations, recreational facilities and transportation to events in other parts of the city. How valuable this is depends a lot on the resident's personality. An active, outgoing person can easily make friends and find interesting things to do; a more private individual may be very isolated even though many people live close by.

One family reluctantly agreed to their mother's choice of a

retirement village, but she found the situation less pleasant than she had hoped.

Rose says, "Mom moved into a retirement residence because things at our house weren't perfect. She complained to her other children about our house: the food, the noise, our outside commitments, the lack of windows, etc. Instead of getting together and working things out, they listened sympathetically to these complaints and eventually persuaded her to move.

"Well, the food was different, there was less noise and there was natural light (she had to keep the shades closed because it hurt her eyes!), but she was never happy there. She missed us and our children, but we could only visit her twice a week. She refused to go to the dining room and paid someone to bring dinner to her instead. She also hired someone to come in each day to help her dress, organize her pills, do a little shopping and cleaning for her. This soon exhausted her financial resources."

Another couple explains why they left such a center. "We just weren't happy there. Things seemed too regimented. For example, for the convenience of the kitchen help, meals on weekends were served earlier than we liked. Then there was nothing going on the rest of the day.

"We felt safe, and we weren't isolated. There were people around all the time, but we found it hard to get around from one part of the complex to another."

Another family had to take their mother out of a village where she wasn't being closely supervised. "All Mom would eat was candy, and it wasn't long before she became ill and emaciated."

One parent made a perceptive comment after living in a retirement village a few months: "There's nobody here but old people!" This can make a person feel she's consigned to a very uninteresting life. It is also depressing when friends and acquaintances decline and die. Each move within the complex seems like a step toward death. A resident may resist each one, but the decision is usually out of her hands. If she cannot care for herself in certain objectively specified ways, she will be moved.

As one woman put it, "You don't come here to live; you come here to die." Ideally, a person who chooses to move into a retirement center should have an optimistic attitude. She can decide to live as full a life as possible, as long as possible. A person who has always been confident and optimistic will usually do well in a retirement village.

Sharing a Home

Although there are other options in individual cases, I strongly believe it is ordinarily God's plan for children to open their own homes to elderly parents who can no longer live alone. Even the most up-to-date institution is no substitute for direct care by loving children.

Love is the only valid reason for opening your home to a parent. By love I don't mean a gushy emotion that may wax and wane, but that unselfishness which sets the other's good above your own, seeking to please God and to do what is best for your parent.

Edna explains the need for this kind of love. "I was eager to care for my grandmother because I loved her very much, but one morning when I was changing yet another soiled sheet I realized my natural love for my grandmother was exhausted. At that point, only love for the Lord could sustain me."

There are less perfect motives for taking in a parent, such as guilt, feeling backed into a corner or a cold sense of obligation. Motives like these provide a starting point, but they cannot sustain you when the going gets rough. God knows your heart and accepts you as you are. If you bring your imperfect motives to him along with your desire to embrace his will, he can transform your heart so that you love his will and find joy in caring for your parent.

Those who wholeheartedly seek to please God and do what is best for their parents will still encounter many obstacles, both within themselves and in the circumstances of their lives. Sometimes these obstacles will make a different course of action necessary, but often they can be overcome by prayer, compromise and the help and support of others.

We have already discussed parental unwillingness. Unless your parent is mentally incompetent, this obstacle is insurmountable unless God changes her heart and leads her to change her mind.

Your ambivalence or unwillingness to care for your parent is discussed under "Past Hurts" in Chapter Four.

Your husband must be wholeheartedly behind any decision to take a parent into your home. He will be able to steer you through a multitude of adjustments, helping you rearrange schedules, space, finances and priorities as necessary. He should shoulder the responsibility with you and be there to support you, especially when the going gets rough. His prayer, example and leadership will help the whole family pull together to make this work. However, if your husband is reluctant or unwilling, caring for a parent in the home will not only be difficult for you but drive a deadly wedge between the two of you.

If you believe you should bring a parent into your home, you and your husband must discuss it thoroughly. After you tell him your concerns and convictions, if he still cannot agree to this step, together you should work out a plan of action you both can accept. Perhaps you can alternate responsibility with siblings. Perhaps you can spend time regularly in your parent's home. Perhaps you can set a definite time as a trial period to see what it would be like to have your parent in your home. You should never act behind your husband's back, however strong your sense of duty toward your parent. If you accept your husband's decision and pray persistently for God's will to be done, you may be surprised to see how the apparent impasse is resolved.

Your children's objections do not have the same weight. By all means, listen to their feelings, ideas and objections. The family should work together to prevent foreseeable difficulties and deal with tensions as they arise. Your children need to know that you love them, want the best for them, still have time for them and want to know how they view the new living situation. However, it is up to you as parents to make the final decision, after weighing your children's input. Once made, it should be supported by every family member, with plenty of parental love and guidance.

Other common objections to taking in a parent include lack

of time, money, space, skill and compatibility. God's grace can help you overcome them all.

Caring for a parent will take a great deal of time, and the demand will probably increase as the parent grows weaker and more ill. It's easy to look at an already bulging schedule and remark, "I don't have time for this."

It's not a matter of freeing up an hour here or there; rather, it's opening your whole life to another person, somewhat like welcoming a new baby into the family. Your husband can often help you see which activities you should drop in order to care for the parent and which you should maintain to keep your spirits up.

Lack of time and money is a more acute issue if you work outside the home. Does this automatically rule out taking in a parent?

Although many women work outside the home, don't assume this is best without taking a careful look at all the factors involved. What would the family lose if you quit your job or cut back your hours in order to care for a parent? Might not the reduction in income be balanced not only by the intangible reward of doing the most generous thing but also by monetary savings on clothing, transportation, hired help and convenience foods? How would this lowered income compare with the cost of paying someone else to take care of your parent? Can she herself make a financial contribution that would offset this reduction in income? Most parents could contribute what they formerly paid for housing and utilities, while their moving in will not greatly increase family living expenses. Many states and insurance plans also provide financial incentives for people who choose to care for parents at home rather than institutionalizing them. Adult day-care centers and paid companions willing to come into homes are also available in many communities.

Of course, not all parents require round-the-clock care. It may be possible for you to continue working, perhaps taking advantage of flex-time to be with your parent during the long, lonely middle of the day. Many jobs can also be done from your own home.

Lack of space can be solved in several ways. It has been our

Where Should They Live?

family's experience that people who are getting along can live happily in tight quarters, while there is no house big enough for those who are at odds with one another! Open communication and relationships full of affection, forbearance and forgiveness are the best space-savers.

However, rearrangement of living space may be necessary. Perhaps the family doesn't need both a living room and a family room. Large rooms can be subdivided for privacy. A closet can be remodeled into a first-floor bathroom.

Building an addition is another option. It could have its own outside entrance, wheelchair access for all rooms, a small kitchenette and a bathroom with safety railings and a shower seat. If heating and cooling units are separate, Mom can maintain the temperature that's comfortable for her. Doors between the addition and the main part of the house could enable you to check easily to make sure Mom hasn't fallen. If they are soundproof, she can turn up the television as loud as she likes and won't have to listen to teenagers' radios. She can easily be part of what's going on in the family, yet she can escape to a quieter place and entertain her friends there in a more intimate setting.

Moving into your parent's home is another possibility. Especially if your parent already lives near you, this may be the most practical option, but it can also be very difficult.

Nicole says, "It made a lot of sense for us to move in with Mom after Dad died. Her house was all on one level, the neighborhood was safe and the mortgage was paid. She knew she couldn't continue to live alone, so she welcomed our coming. I had no idea how hard this would be for me!

"Except for our bedrooms, we kept Mom's furniture and put ours in the basement or in storage. This seemed like the sensible thing to do, but sometimes I feel homesick for my own things. When my son comes home from college, he immediately heads for the basement where the familiar furniture is.

"It's hard adjusting to another person's method and routine for housecleaning. Mom wants the living room dusted a lot more often than I, but she doesn't seem to notice the places that need plastering. It took us a long time to persuade her to replace some very worn wallpaper.

"All the clichés about two women sharing a kitchen are true! We each like to cook in our own pots, and we don't agree about which meals are served on china and which on Corelle. I still have trouble finding what I want in her pantry.

"Even more difficult are life-style questions that affect our children. Since it's her home, I feel awkward asking her to turn off a soap opera I don't want the children to overhear. We finally compromised on this one by moving her television into her sitting room and making that off-limits to the children, but issues like that arise from time to time.

"I know it must be even harder for Mom to adjust to our ways. For years, she had only Dad to pick up after. Now all of a sudden her home is full of our clutter. Putting myself in her shoes helps me to be more understanding. I try to do things her way as often as possible, but I also find that when I approach her respectfully she's very open to rearranging things according to my logic."

Instead of remodeling an existing house, you and Mom may be able to sell your separate houses and build or buy a house together. You can decide together what kind of home you want, in what neighborhood, and how to arrange things in the house.

It's wise to discuss this with sisters and brothers before taking action, since it means tying up much of what would otherwise be their inheritance. Before moving, Mom may give special pieces of furniture to her other children. This makes more space in the new home; it's also a tangible reminder of her love for each child.

I saw this work for a friend whose mother was gravely ill. Despite her limitations, they involved her as much as possible in the decision process, bringing her samples of carpet and wallpaper when she couldn't go out shopping. She didn't live very long after their move, but their new home is full of precious memories of her.

What if you feel incapable of taking care of a parent, especially one with a specific illness or disability? You may think you'd be terrified to give insulin injections, have oxygen in the house, make your mother do physical therapy, empty her catheter bag or even give her a bath. If you're willing to learn, though, most communities have teaching resources for care-

Where Should They Live?

givers. Ask the local hospital. The Visiting Nurses' Association also provides nursing services, teaches caregivers how to perform simple tasks and checks back regularly to make sure medical equipment is functioning properly.

Differences in life-style may seem insurmountable. For example, what if the parent likes to watch television all day while the children in the family have had their television viewing carefully monitored and restricted? Conversely, what if the grandparent disapproves of television shows the grandchildren are used to watching?

We will discuss some of these specifics in Chapter Six; none of them precludes sharing a home. With goodwill and respect on both sides, you can reach creative compromises. Few questions of life-style are matters of right and wrong. Far from compromising family principles, deferring to an older person's preferences serves to reinforce the family's commitment to charity.

In summary, welcoming a parent into your home is neither easy nor trouble-free; it may be the greatest challenge you've ever faced! Moments of agony and moments of bliss occur, but both are far less frequent than sheer hard work. Any such change requires major adjustments in attitudes and priorities as well as in schedules and living space.

Whether the adjustments are great or small, sudden or gradual, offering long-term hospitality is the basic commitment within which specifics must be handled.

Moving into a Nursing Home

A nursing home should ordinarily be viewed as a last resort. Because wages are low and working conditions far from ideal, there tends to be a lot of turnover in nursing-home personnel. Many are good-hearted but untrained. Others may be skilled technicians but cold and inconsiderate toward the people for whom they care. Even more alarming, abuse of residents, rape or attempted rape are not unheard of.

Even if staff members are competent and compassionate, the resident-to-staff ratio is inevitably higher than in a home where one older person lives with a couple or a whole family who can be attentive to her needs. This means that the nursing-home residents who get the most attention are the ones with the most disruptive behavior or the most acute medical needs; those who don't make a fuss and demand attention usually don't get it. They may sit for hours in the same position in front of a television tuned to programs they don't like. They may be wet or soiled, even if they could have used the restroom with assistance. Perhaps they are restrained, tied to a chair, ostensibly for their own safety but also to protect the facility from lawsuit if they were to get up and injure themselves.

Nevertheless, there are circumstances in which a nursing home is the best or the only alternative. A daughter describes one such situation.

"I vowed I would never put my mother in a nursing home! As my widowed mother grew older, I tried to persuade her to move closer to my family in another state, but she was very independent and couldn't stand the thought of leaving the neighborhood where she had grown up, married and raised her children. Then the dreaded day came. She suffered a massive stroke and cerebral hemorrhage that left her partially paralyzed. The hospital social worker called me into her office and told me Mom could linger on for years. She asked which nursing home we wanted to move her into.

"I tried to arrange for an airplane ambulance to transport her to my home, but no doctor would sign a release for this; her health was too frail. I put her into the best nursing home I could find and returned home without her. I visit as often as I can, but every time I have to leave her it's difficult. It never gets easier. I will never again judge another person harshly for putting a parent into a nursing home. Sometimes there's just no alternative!"

A nursing home may also become necessary when a parent requires skilled nursing care such as intravenous feeding. If a doctor, nurse or social worker advises this, do not hesitate to ask questions so you can evaluate whether it's really necessary. Find out, too, whether the placement can be temporary or needs to be long-term. Some medical conditions for which hospitalization used to be mandatory can now be treated at home with the right kind of instruction, equipment and super-

Where Should They Live?

vision. However, a doctor might not suggest this unless you indicate your interest in doing it.

The family should also discuss how much medical intervention is desirable in case of a terminal illness. Is nursing-home care necessary for the parent's recovery or comfort, or will it just be a more impersonal setting for prolonging her dying?

Sometimes caring for a parent in the home is either a physical impossibility (perhaps a bedridden parent is too heavy to lift) or such an emotional strain that it threatens the integrity of the family. In these hard cases, a nursing home may be the only loving choice.

A daughter says, "As my mother's illness progressed, she needed round-the-clock care. We weren't able to give her that. At the same time, she became increasingly fearful and clung to us. How difficult it was to leave her in a nursing home! It would never have been her choice, yet we felt we were doing the loving thing, the right thing for her, not selfishly looking out for our own interests.

"We gave her a great deal of emotional support during and after this transition. We tried not to take her complaints personally but to respond kindly to her fears and concerns, to give her our loving attention."

It's a good idea to discuss this option with your parent before a crisis forces a decision. Claire says, "Mom and I have discussed nursing homes. She has a no-nonsense approach. She says, 'If you need to put me into a nursing home at some point, do it! Don't listen to me if I wail and complain. I know you love me.'"

Choosing the right nursing home is not easy. Here are some questions to ask.

Is the facility licensed, along with its personnel?

Is it clean throughout?

Is the staff courteous and knowledgeable? How do they treat residents? Is the atmosphere homelike?

Are there enough staff members to take care of patients without making them feel rushed?

Does it have a fire/smoke detection system, security against crime, emergency call buttons in each room and adequate emergency exits?

How is the food? Is there variety? A nutritional balance? Is the environment free of barriers?

Is there an outdoor recreation area? Is it safe?

Are physicians and other health-care professionals—therapists, for example—readily available?

Are there planned activities such as religious services, recreation, crafts, field trips, things to do on weekends and evenings as well as during the day?

Is it easy for people to come visit? Can the resident get where she might need or want to go (doctors, beautician, entertainment, church, shopping)?

What does it cost, and what methods of payment are accepted?

Are there additional services such as a beauty shop? Does a telephone cost extra?

Is privacy ensured, especially in bedrooms, bathrooms, lounges and public telephone areas?

Does the resident have access to her own money?

Sarah says, "I almost chose the wrong nursing home. I visited several, and the one I liked best at first was the one with the most pleasant entrance area. It was clean and uncluttered, and I liked the sense of order.

"As I investigated further, I learned that my state rates nursing homes annually. Another facility in our town was rated higher in terms of nursing care, and I realized this was more important to my mother in the long run than appearance. When I returned for a second visit to the better-rated nursing home, I realized why I hadn't been so impressed with its entranceway. The area wasn't designed to impress visitors; it was actually used by the residents. No wonder it looked more cluttered! This home had a sense of freedom, and was an environment where my mother was in fact very happy.

"I had visited another facility with the proverbial urine stench and dirty floors. I knew that wasn't what I wanted for my mother!"

Besides gathering information, it's important for both you and your parent to visit the nursing home. A facility which meets all the criteria may still not feel right; take your instinctive reactions seriously!

Where Should They Live?

Helping your mother get the best possible care in a nursing home is discussed in Chapter Seven. Nursing-home administrators recommend getting on the waiting list at your chosen facility before the need arises. Otherwise, a bed may not be available when you need it.

CHAPTER SIX

Welcoming a Parent Into Your Home

The basic decision for parent and child to share a home is only the beginning; many other decisions must follow. Some can be foreseen, others will arise as life together unfolds.

Ideally, the mother should sit down first with her daughter and son-in-law, then with their whole family, to discuss what this change will mean to all of them. What modifications are needed to make the house suitable for two or three generations? How will each person's life change? How do they feel about those changes?

Clear agreements should be made about living space, finances and division of labor. Many families find it helpful to put these agreements in writing.

Here are some specific issues to talk about.

Housing Arrangements

What are mother's specific disabilities, and how should the home be modified for her? If she has trouble seeing, you may need to improve lighting, especially in hallways and on stairs. Reflective tape can be used to mark sharp corners, steps or other changes in levels. If she is unsteady on her feet, you should remove throw rugs, unclutter passageways, install handrails even on short flights of steps and attach grab rails to tub and toilet. If she can't handle stairs, there should be a first-floor bathroom and bedroom (or alternatives such as a stair-glide elevator). Doorways and halls may need to be widened if she uses a wheelchair.

Older people tend to become chilled easily because of circulatory problems and weight loss. As my mother-in-law says, "I don't have much meat on my bones." However, I can't stand to keep the house as warm as she wants it, and I shudder to think of the hike in our heating bill.

We try to keep certain areas of the house warm for Mom. A space heater in her bedroom at night can be moved into the bathroom when she bathes. When she's in the rest of the house, she puts on an extra layer or two and wraps up in a warm but lightweight stadium blanket. Knee warmers, bed socks and winter underwear also help keep her warm. On a gloomy day, we close the curtains; on a sunny day, having them open makes her feel warmer. In the winter, she doesn't like a cold drink with her meals but prefers a cup of tea or a bowl of soup. A moderate amount of exercise helps her circulation. We joke a lot about living at the North Pole and envision heaven as having a balmy tropical climate all year round.

Paying attention to details can make a big difference. It's hard for Mom to get comfortable. She doesn't have much padding and can get really sore sitting on a hard chair. On the other hand, she has a hard time getting out of a chair that's too soft!

She tested recliner chairs until she found a comfortable one to purchase. Other family members can use it, but they understand they have to move when Grandma wants to sit there. We also use a seat cushion on her dining-room chair and try to remember to bring it during long car rides, when we're going to church or to places with hard seats. We've even carried a rocking chair to some events. It's a place of honor for her and a conversation-starter!

If remodeling or construction is necessary, how much will it cost? Are you satisfied not only with the price but with how this will change your home?

Will your mother's coming shift children to other rooms or make them double up? How will they handle that?

Welcoming a Parent into Your Home

How can you make her feel at home in the common areas as well as in her own room or apartment? What will she do with her own furniture?

Bobbie says, "I know it was hard for Mom to move into my home. For years, she was the homemaker, the one I went to for advice. Although she expressed approval of my choices and my abilities, moving into a home where I was the woman of the house was very difficult for her.

"The house was already organized according to my system and filled with my family's possessions. We tried to make room for as many of her things as possible, but this didn't make the home hers. She's very gracious about it, but I know it must be a strain always feeling like a stranger, or even a beloved guest.

"I try to respect her preferences as much as possible. She's arranged her own bedroom and sitting room. She doesn't have a separate kitchen, but I've freed a cupboard for her special things and I try to keep on hand the ingredients she likes to cook with. Whenever a change is needed in the house, even a new coat of paint, we try to involve her in the discussion and decision-making. We consult her about preparations for special occasions. Her ideas, hopes, likes and dislikes are very important to us."

Finances

Many families find it helpful to have a written agreement about finances. Can she make a regular monthly contribution? Can she underwrite the cost of remodeling, or should this cost be split? Does she expect to continue paying her own medical expenses and insurance? Will her insurance coverage need to change?

Norma says, "Before Mom moved in, we drew up a written contract specifying our financial responsibilities and hers. This cleared the air and made things very peaceful. We all know exactly where we stand.

"I have a friend whose mother occasionally leaves $10 lying on the table and feels she's done her share. I'm sure she has no idea what it costs to run the household and what hidden expenses she's caused: buying food for her special diet, keeping the heat set higher because she gets chilled so easily, installing faucets her arthritic hands can turn, transporting her to appointments. My friend is glad to do all these things, but she wishes they'd entered into a financial arrangement before her mother moved in; she's afraid bringing it up now would offend her."

On the other hand, Ceil says, "Mom doesn't make a regular contribution to our household. It was her decision. Before she moved in, we laid out what we felt it would cost us to have her there. We asked her to pray about her contribution and told her we would respect whatever she decided. We preferred leaving it up to her rather than requiring a specific amount.

"At first, her decision not to pay regular rent made me uncomfortable and somewhat anxious about our finances. I had to let go of that anxiety, trust God to provide for our needs, and open my eyes to the very real contribution Mom was making. In fact, she's very generous with us. If she sees a need, she takes the initiative to meet it, for example, replacing worn furniture or buying a new set of pots and pans. She just doesn't want to be tied down."

Meals

How much does your mother want to be integrated with the rest of the family? Will she take all her meals with you, or would she prefer to have a separate kitchenette? If this isn't possible, would she like to prepare or eat her meals at different times so she can have more privacy and maintain her customary diet? If she plans to eat with the family, does she want to be involved in meal planning and preparation? Are there things that need to be included in her diet, either for medical reasons or by habit and preference? Can the whole family make these modifications? On the other hand, is Mom willing or able to eat the way the family already eats? Will separate meals or portions be necessary? Should you set aside some food before it is salted or sugared?

I never dreamed how much Mom's presence would affect our diet. She isn't a picky eater, but she's used to a more limited variety of foods and cooking styles than we are. She often bites

Welcoming a Parent into Your Home

her lip or gets sores in her mouth and generally can't tolerate foods that are acidic, too hard, too stringy or seedy.

At first, our children were quite vocal about what they considered a terrible injustice! How could we insist they eat their beets when Grandma never had to eat hers? Why did we save the whole milk for her and serve them powdered milk? Why did they have to earn dessert by finishing their supper while there were always sweets for her?

We tried to help them understand something about Grandma's life experience as well as her present limitations. We encouraged them to ask her questions, for example, about what her family had for dinner every Sunday and how they made do during the Depression. We explained that it was hard for her not to be able to eat some of the foods she used to enjoy because of her stomach and her teeth. We promised them that, by the time they reach 88, no one will force them to eat what they don't like!

For my part, I've had to accept the fact that Mom doesn't want much variety in her diet. She's perfectly content eating the same thing for breakfast and lunch every day. As long as it's nutritionally balanced, why should I try to change her preferences? I just try to keep her favorite foods on hand. A friend suggested a simple way to provide a hot breakfast: put milk on her cereal, then warm it in the microwave. For dinner, I haven't altered my menu planning much, but I do try to look at each meal and make sure she can eat it without too much difficulty. Sometimes that means cooking a portion of the omelet without vegetables, making some plain cookies before putting in the nuts, or baking a potato and melting a little cheese on it.

A friend whose mother is somewhat more independent handles things differently. She gives her mother a copy of the menus at the beginning of each week. If there's something her mother would rather not eat, she simply fixes her own alternative that evening on a hot plate in her apartment.

Chores

Is your mother willing and able to share the household workload? Does she want to take a regular turn at cooking, dishwashing and cleaning, or would she prefer to pitch in as her energy permits? Putting her on a regular schedule for chores may help her budget her energy. However, if that energy varies greatly from day to day, keeping such commitments may be more burdensome than simply volunteering to help when she's feeling able.

Most parents like to make a tangible contribution, however small. Someone who can't walk may still be able to fold laundry or to peel potatoes. Even if she can't do these jobs as rapidly as others, it's important to give her opportunities to do what she can and to thank her for what she does.

For example, Marlene says, "Mom's a pro at making applesauce. I bought a bushel of apples, and that kept her busy for a month! We all cheer her on. She also spends one day a week cutting coupons for me, helps with the grocery list and planning meals."

Greta says, "My mother is so supportive! If I leave a load of laundry in the dryer, I come home to find it folded. When I'm cooking, she's quietly washing dishes to keep my work space clear. She loves to find just the right touch for our home: a colorful bouquet for the table, a new utensil to replace a worn one. I have to be careful to thank her, rather than taking all this for granted!

"Even more than all this practical help, I know my mother is on my side. She doesn't say much, but I can tell by her expression and her squeezing my arm that she understands how difficult it is to manage the complex schedules of a busy household, parent a teenage son who challenges my authority, and know what to say to a troubled friend. She doesn't step in without being invited, but I can turn to her for advice when I need it. She's come through similar experiences in her own life so graciously, it gives me a great deal of hope."

Baby-Sitting

Another question to discuss is baby-sitting. Is she willing and able to baby-sit, or do you need to make other arrangements? Does she herself need someone with her all the time? Briege shares her experience.

Welcoming a Parent into Your Home

"Mom gave us many hours of free baby-sitting while her health was still good. However, I had to be careful not to take advantage of her generosity, not to assume she could do this without asking her, and to be sensitive to when the children were just too much for her. Sometimes my husband and I took turns going to meetings, or we would go late so we could tuck the children in before we left.

"As she has become weaker, the situation has reversed. Now, even though our children can care for themselves or are going with us, we have to find someone to stay with Grandma. We stop to consider whether the child in charge that evening can help her get ready for bed. When we've had to go out of town, someone in the household has usually been able to stay with Mom, but one weekend no one could. We wanted another widow to come spend the nights, but how could we explain this to Mom without hurting her feelings?

"I finally told her, 'Mom, this is something we need to do for our own peace of mind. We just don't feel comfortable leaving you in the house by yourself. Is it all right with you if Hilda comes around suppertime and spends nights here while we're away? That will help us enjoy the wedding without worrying about what's happening at home.'"

Outside Help

This brings up another issue. How much help will your family need? Where can you find help, and who will pay for it? Is skilled nursing care necessary? Are there things family members need to learn to do themselves? If she needs someone with her all the time, can members of the extended family share this responsibility, or will extra care be necessary? Are there friends or professional aides who will come into the home? Does the town have an adult day-care facility and does this seem like a good environment for her, either on a regular or occasional basis?

One family found that Medicaid would pay for professional nursing services, and the mother's savings allowed her to hire a companion while her daughter was at work during the day. However, they faced a crisis when more costly night care became a necessity as well. If someone wasn't keeping vigil all night, she would quietly get up at midnight and dress for the day. One night the family didn't hear her until she fell and awakened them. At that point, they put her into a nursing home.

Paula tells how she slowly realized her need for help in caring for her mother and how she is working at finding this help. "I was afraid to leave my mother alone. She has osteoporosis and I was afraid she'd fall and break something. She also gets very anxious when I'm not around. Her need for me was obvious, but I was beginning to feel very closed in, as if I had no life of my own.

"I finally realized having me with her 24 hours a day wasn't good for Mom any more than it was good for me. I had nothing to share with her and no reserves of affection to sweeten my care for her. I began to view time away from the house as a renewal rather than an escape. After a long telephone conversation with my brother who lives out of state, we agreed that he would pay for a companion to relieve me in caring for Mom several times a week.

"When friends asked how they could support me, I used to say, 'I'm managing fine.' Now I ask if they can spend a few hours with Mom either regularly or occasionally. She enjoys having visitors and it gives me a break.

"Since I'm over 55, Mom and I qualify for the senior discount on art and continuing-education classes. Doing things like these together gets us both out and gives us new skills, interests and friends."

Outings

How a parent will spend her time is another important issue to discuss before she moves in. Will the family need to help keep her occupied, or is she able to get out on her own? If she is active and alert, welcoming her into your household will not be as emotionally draining and time-consuming, but there will have to be a lot of give and take.

This is what Bobbie says about her mother. "She has her own life outside the family: friends, church, clubs, volunteer

Welcoming a Parent into Your Home

work, recreation. Sometimes she forgets to tell me she's not coming home for dinner or is bringing a guest. Sometimes I forget to inform her about my plans, too. Fortunately, we've been able to laugh when these oversights cause unforeseen problems.

"Sometimes we have conflicting expectations and needs. She may want to relax in front of the television in the evening, preferably in my company, while I expect quiet so I can supervise the children's homework. I may assume I should wash her linens with the family wash, while she would prefer to do her own laundry. Some of these differences are easy to resolve; others not so easy."

Naomi's mother can also still get out. Naomi says, "As Mom gets more frail, I see more of a need to get her out of the house, even if it's only to go to the store with me, so that her world doesn't close in on her. I also see more of a need to sit down and visit with her, just to be with her, for example, as she eats her lunch.

"I spend a lot of time driving her places. Because of a foot injury, she's no longer able to drive or to negotiate public transportation, nor are buses as handy in our small town as they were in the city where she grew up.

"She has many physical ailments which require visits to different doctors, but there's nothing wrong with her mental faculties, so she likes to handle as much as possible of her own banking, shopping and other affairs. This winds up taking a great deal of my time.

"I've always hated to shop. I try to organize my life to combine as many errands as possible. Instead of browsing, I like to enter a store with a very specific objective in mind, go straight to that part of the store and find what I want.

"My mother's errands are not only numerous but also time-consuming; visits to the bank, the beautician and her favorite snack shop can easily stretch into hours. For her, shopping is a pleasure to be savored in a leisurely fashion. She likes to chat with the clerks and linger over her selections. Just finding the right greeting card can take up half a day.

"Quite honestly, I often resent these long excursions. Sometimes I can combine my own errands with hers, and sometimes she accepts my suggestion of an easier way to do things, such as banking or buying postage stamps by mail.

"However, I have to understand that her objective isn't simply to accomplish specific tasks but to make her life more varied and interesting. If I didn't drive her around, she'd be absolutely homebound and have much less control over her own life. I try to set aside my own preferences and chauffeur her willingly. If I were in her place, I wouldn't want to stay home and watch television all day either!"

If your mother is bedridden or severely memory-impaired, your family's life may come to revolve around her needs. This will cause major changes in life-style, routines and relationships.

Anne Marie's mother is housebound, but "I try to give her as much freedom of choice as possible. Even though she can't get out independently, she still has preferences! If she needs a new dress, I bring home three from the store on approval so she can try them on and decide on one. I buy boxed greeting cards so she can select one and send it with a little money to each family member celebrating a special occasion. I ask what she wants for breakfast or lunch. I try to act as her sister, not her mother, in areas like these."

Life-Style

Differing expectations and life-styles can cause great and small problems. For example, what if prayer is an ordinary part of the family's life, while your mother uses God's name only as an expletive?

As parents, you're responsible for setting the tone for what goes on in your family. It can be tricky to respect and honor your parents yet take proper responsibility for setting house rules and making sure everyone is relating in a loving way. Parents shouldn't compromise what they judge to be essential just because the grandparent objects. While religion can't be forced on your parent, she should normally be expected to refrain from profanity, at least in front of the grandchildren.

I can get very irritated and self-righteous when Mom's preferences seem to make extra work for me or to alter our life-

Welcoming a Parent into Your Home

style. Many examples seem trivial in the telling. We're committed to recycling, but she won't use a washable handkerchief. She goes through boxes of Kleenex instead. (I have a friend who prefers tissues, but her mother won't part with her lace handkerchief!) Since she's been with us we've had to drive places we used to bike to. She insists on eating with a spoon instead of a fork and always needs a knife to cut her food into tinier pieces. She wants the holes in her socks darned instead of buying a new pair. She likes to peel potatoes but she can't use a peeler and I dislike seeing her cut off so much of the vegetable with a paring knife.

Silverware once led Vicky to an important realization. She always used to set the table with just a fork, and it annoyed her when her mother asked for a knife and spoon. Then one day her husband asked, "Why don't you just give her a knife and spoon in the first place?" She realized God was asking her to accept her mother as she was, with her idiosyncrasies, preferences and harmless habits.

How unreasonable and selfish I often am! How can I expect Mom to change the way she's done things for 80 years, especially when she's been willing to give up her independence and so many of her preferences to come live with us in the first place!

What simple, everyday opportunities to follow Jesus' command to die to myself, my ways and preferences! Sometimes I even discover new skills or new values in the process. There's a precious story to explain most of Mom's preferences, stories of using up a bumper crop of tomatoes or imitating a favorite relative. By doing things her way, I'm not only honoring her but building lifetime memories for my own family.

A little perspective makes humor possible. For months I fumed silently because Mom persisted in throwing used toilet paper into the wastebasket instead of the toilet—until I talked with a friend who had to keep calling a plumber because his mother plugged up the toilet with paper!

There isn't always an ideal solution. Cathy says her father's smoking is a real problem. "Smoke really bothers several members of our household. We've encouraged Dad to stop smoking but it's unrealistic to insist on something that would be so difficult for him. Instead, he confines smoking to his room and outdoors. We try to make sure cigarettes and matches are safely extinguished without hovering over him all the time. This is just something we're learning to live with."

Most matters of life-style call for compromise rather than firmness. Personal taste affects everyone's TV-viewing and musical preferences, so some entertainment should be confined to certain hours or to certain rooms, for example. Menus can be varied to accommodate individual preferences. Love really can overcome all obstacles, and compromises arranged with love can enrich everyone in the household.

Understanding

There are bound to be tensions in merging two households and two or more generations. All potential conflicts can't be resolved in advance, but it's helpful to understand what each person expects of others in the household and to talk in a general way about the need for open communication, humility and forgiveness when things don't work as well as everyone intends.

Try to understand how difficult it is for your parent to give up treasured independence, especially if the move is being made because she is no longer able to care for herself as she has always done. Besides giving up her familiar home and furniture, her independence and her privacy, she's facing new losses daily as her friends die, her health declines and her strength fades.

Fran says, "The more I do for Mom, the more irritated she gets with me! When she doesn't seem to appreciate my service, it's easy for me to be resentful and irritated with her.

"Two things have helped me. One is something God did for me one evening. I was carrying in a basin of water to soak her toes before clipping her nails (no small task!). I was doing the right thing, but I was grumbling inside until Jesus reminded me, 'When you touch her feet, realize that you are really washing my feet.' My resentment melted into love and gratitude. I try to remember this every time I have a chance to serve her. Having to lay down my life for her has shown me clearly how small my heart is, how reluctant I am to put my life at another's disposal, how much I disdain small, unheralded service.

Welcoming a Parent into Your Home

"The other thing was realizing how difficult it is for her to have to ask for help with things she used to be able to handle herself. It's a sign that she's growing older and weaker, a real loss of independence. The more she needs me, the more resentful she feels. She isn't really upset with me; I'm just a humiliating reminder of her own weakness.

"Now I try to walk a fine line, letting her do as much as she can for herself but trying to intervene before she becomes frustrated. I unobtrusively anticipate her needs so she doesn't have to ask for help. A sense of humor also helps overcome embarrassment. I'll say, 'If you'd just play the exercise tape on the VCR instead of watching the news, you could bend down and clip your own toenails!' She'll respond, 'How about speeding up that exercise tape next time?' "

Most parents' greatest fear is that they will be a burden. Few people are as humble as Frieda, who says, "I try not to worry about being a burden to those I live with. God has put us together in this situation, and I figure it's for their benefit as well as mine!" By your own attitude, you can help your parent feel like a blessing rather than a burden. Well-meaning friends may offer you sympathy for "bearing this cross."

Gloria disagrees. "I'm no martyr, and I'm not doing anything extraordinary. I'm just doing my best to take care of my mother. It's not a cross, it's an opportunity to love and serve God and her. Sure, it's difficult at times, but I rely on God's promise that I can do all things in his strength (Ph. 4:13). I also rely on his love, so wonderfully described in 1 Corinthians 13:1-7."

Your caregiving role is likely to expand as your parent ages. It's perfectly natural to experience exhaustion, boredom, frustration, anger and guilt at your own inadequacy. Acknowledge these reactions, share them with your husband, pastor or close friend, and bring them to God in prayer. Paula advises, "Be sure you want to care for your mom. If you don't, and feel victimized or a martyr, either get your feelings straightened out or change the situation, because she'll surely pick up on your feelings."

Again and again, children caring for parents in their homes say, "The little things are the hardest." Alison says, "I always rise to the occasion when there's a crisis, but the little things wear me down. My husband says if the house was burning down around me I'd be a pillar of strength, but if someone spills a glass of milk I go to pieces! How hard it's been for me to allow extra time for Mom to get up out of her chair, put on her coat and get into the car, for example!

"I know, of course, that I can't live from crisis to crisis. I have to be available for Mom in the day-to-day details of living together. The truth of the Incarnation has become increasingly meaningful to me: I know God is with us in the smallest things as well as the most important.

"It helps to be aware of my weakness in this area, but I haven't experienced instant transformation. Again and again I have to ask Mom's forgiveness for my sharp words, hurried actions and neglect. We've made an agreement. When she notices me losing it, she'll say, 'Don't sweat the small stuff!' Being able to laugh at myself at moments like these helps a lot."

Personal Care

What if your mother has trouble accepting personal care from you? Anita says, "Mom didn't want me to bathe her or give her personal care. 'Why do you have to do this?,' she asked. I answered, 'Because I love you and I'm trying to serve God by caring for you.' As she felt more secure in our love, she became more accepting of this kind of service. We try to meet all Mom's needs and as many of her wants as possible, and she has become very content. In fact, Mom's personality changed after she had been living with us for a while. Up till that point, she had been difficult and demanding. Once she decided she really wanted to be with us, she became very peaceful."

I've learned a lot of practical things about personal care. A nurse friend recommended rubbing Sea Breeze antiseptic into Mom's scalp when it starts to get dry and scaly; it smells refreshing and isn't greasy. I didn't know how to shampoo her hair without getting water in her ears; someone suggested using lamb's wool (available with foot-care supplies in a pharmacy) instead of cotton balls, lubricating the wool with petroleum jelly. There is also dry shampoo you can rub in and brush out.

Vaseline is better than most skin creams. I rub it into Mom's dry skin to keep it more supple. Her skin is thin and tears easily, and a bandage often irritates it, so I try to keep wounds clean with hydrogen peroxide and antibiotic ointment but leave them uncovered to heal. Taking vitamin C is supposed to make the skin a little stronger and able to heal faster.

When baths became difficult to manage, friends made two suggestions. One was to place a plastic chair in the shower and have Mom sit down while I soap her all over. Another was to sit her on the toilet, fill a basin with water and uncover only a small part of her body at a time, patting her dry before moving on to the next area.

Suggestions like these are often given at seminars for caregivers offered by hospitals, adult daycare centers and other service organizations. I also discovered an informal network of caregivers in my town. One person introduced me to another, and if I had a specific question they could usually think of someone who had solved a similar problem.

Schedule

How will you handle the schedule conflicts that are part of the "small stuff"? Naomi says, "Mom isn't on the same schedule as the rest of us. Because of her physical limitations, it's hard for her to get up and get going in the morning. She likes to sleep quite late, then have breakfast in bed. She likes to watch TV into the late evening, when she's always wakeful. She'd really like us to sit down and watch with her, but, of course, this doesn't match well with the schedule we need to follow to get to work and school on time.

"At first, I expected her to follow our schedule. I tried to make her go to bed at what seemed a reasonable hour and to drag her out of bed in the morning. I told her she wouldn't have such a hard time getting up if she'd only go to bed earlier! That only got us upset with each other; there was no real change.

"Finally I decided I wasn't likely to change longstanding habits which might have some physiological basis. I try to make sure she's up to get her medicine, but other than that I respect her inner clock. I usually have some quiet time to myself after my husband and children leave the house in the morning. Then I bring Mom breakfast in bed and we have some leisurely moments together.

"I try to take advantage of Mom's best time of day, even though it isn't the same as mine. It takes her a long time to get her body going in the morning. However, by late afternoon she's at her best, ready for an outing. She likes to walk out to get the mail, to go out for frozen yogurt, grocery shopping or to the mall. I've tried to rearrange my life so I'm free at her best time to do what she wants to do, or to include her in an outing.

"Then, in the evening, I make sure everything she needs to get ready for bed is set out. She can stay up as long as she likes, but I no longer stay up with her. At first she was somewhat manipulative in trying to engage me in late-night conversation. We dealt with it by having my husband go in with me to say goodnight and then insist that I leave with him, with light-hearted references to my beauty sleep.

"The schedule we've adopted allows Mom to avoid the confusion of everyone getting ready in the morning. Then she's alert when we talk at the supper table."

Sometimes a parent can compromise in matters like this, but often you must accept her as she is.

Time Management

How will you find time to care for your parent the way you want to? All caregivers seem to experience a time crunch. Melissa says, "I told my husband, 'This just isn't working. I'm exhausted. There aren't enough hours in the day to take care of Mom's personal needs, take her to all her appointments, keep up with the housework, cooking and laundry and all the children's demands.' He answered, 'You're not the only one who lives in this house, dirties laundry or eats meals! We all need to pitch in and help.' He asked me to write down the essential tasks of each day, week and month, then we divided them up. We found that Mom herself felt better when we asked her to do some household tasks, even if she couldn't do them as quickly as I could. Our children took turns staying with her while I ran errands. One daughter really enjoyed washing and setting her

Welcoming a Parent into Your Home

hair every week. Everyone learned to do laundry, and we set up a rotating schedule so everyone took a turn cooking meals and cleaning specific areas of the house."

If you work outside the home, you'll have even more of a time crunch. Nicole says, "My mother is in good health and does help with meals, laundry and gardening. However, I feel very stretched some days. After work, there isn't much of me left to give and I just don't have the energy to chat.

"Sometimes, when I come home, I feel like we're playing 20 Questions. My mother follows me from room to room asking about my day. At that point, there are a hundred things I need to do, and it's easy for me to resent her curiosity!

"During the day, she watches game shows on television and does a little housework, but she really doesn't have much to share with me. She isn't able to get out as much as she used to. Perhaps she participates in life partly through me.

"My husband and I have talked about this. We're exploring ways to get Mom out of the house during the day, perhaps through adult daycare, the Harvest House group at church or continuing-education courses at our community college.

"In the meantime, I've tried dealing with my resentment in several ways. Sometimes I tell her I need some quiet time, go into my room and close the door. Prayer does help me get things in perspective, and she can respect this need.

"Sometimes, instead of coming straight home, I stop to do an errand or two. (I call and let her know when to expect me.) This gives me a little time to unwind. On my way home, I try to shift gears from work to home. What can I share with Mom? What do I absolutely need to take care of the minute I get home, and what can wait till later? How can I shift the conversation to her? Perhaps she has nothing worth mentioning from her day, but is there a memory she would share if I asked the right question? For example, a telephone conversation at work could remind me of that trip Mom once took to Georgia, so I can ask her about that.

"Then, when I walk through the door, I try to be genuinely grateful that my mother is there to greet me, and I convey this warmth to her."

Time is valuable, and there's never enough of it. I have so much to do! But what do all my projects matter in comparison with love? What good is all I do for Mom if I don't do it with love and personal attention? What a precious opportunity I have to help prepare her for eternity by loving her and letting her love me now!

All time is God's time; I have to trust that he loans me enough of it to do his will. It's easy to miss the most important thing unless I stay in touch with him and listen to the nudges he gives me. Then, "I don't have time . . . " can change to "Yes, Lord."

One vital consideration is time for you as a married couple to be together without interruption. You need to share what's going on in your expanded household and be sure you agree about how to handle everything. Your husband can support you in practical ways and offer perspective and balance to help you grow and serve your parent better. Beyond this specific need, however, spend time deepening your relationship as husband and wife, which is likely to endure beyond the time your mother lives with you. If necessary, hire a sitter for her so you can get out of the house together.

Retirement may pose new challenges. Doreen says, "When my husband retired, I felt like a yo-yo. As long as he was working, Mother and I had things comfortably worked out. We did some things together and some things separately, and that was never a problem. Now that my husband is around all the time, Mom sometimes seems to resent his claims on my time. 'Are you two going out again?,' she'll ask. 'When are you going to spend some time with me?'

"Sometimes I'm pretty direct with her. 'Yes, we're going out. That's what wives and husbands do!' Other times, we're able to include her in the outing and wish we'd thought of that before she asked.

"I schedule time for each important person in my life so that I don't neglect anyone. My husband and I like to take early morning walks together. Mom and I have agreed to go out for lunch once a week and to invite friends in once a month. On this day, my husband makes other plans for the noon hour."

Grandchildren

How will it work for your parent to share a home with her grandchildren if they are still at home?

Although they are growing toward maturity and unselfishness, at times children of all ages are bound to resent having to share their home with a grandparent, especially if that grandparent is ill or confused, tries to tell them what to do, or restricts their choices. For example, because of Grandma a child may have to give up his bedroom, play more quietly or not entertain as many friends, either because Grandma can't tolerate a lot of noise and activity or because she embarrasses the child in front of his friends.

Sometimes children express anger because they are sensitive and frustrated. Perhaps they don't understand Grandma's illness. They may be keenly aware of how much she has declined physically or mentally and have a hard time accepting the fact that they are powerless to halt this decline.

Help your children get beyond their feelings and learn practical ways to be attentive to Grandma and help care for her. For example, we encourage our children to check in with Grandma when they come home from school, to show her the work they've brought home, tell her something about their day and see if she'd like to listen to the radio with them or hear them recite something they're memorizing for school. A friend's young daughters love to watch Lawrence Welk on Grandma's television and dance for her. Even our preschooler has learned to tell Grandma where she's going and when she'll be back. She loves to fetch Grandma's lap robe or offer her hand to escort her to the dinner table. We don't force the children to do things for her but tell them they should only serve her if they can do it with love. Of course, she often rewards their service with pocket change, so perhaps their motives are less than pure!

The children know they have to knock on her door and wait for her to let them in, rather than barging in unannounced. Sometimes she is too tired to entertain them. They've had to learn to face her and speak clearly so she can understand what they're saying. In all these ways they've become more courteous, that is, more kind and attentive to another person's needs.

Despite what our children perceive as inconveniences, John and I are convinced that caring for his mother in our home is beneficial for them. They have moved beyond the stereotype of grandmas as sweet old ladies with full cookie jars. Their grandma is a real person who likes swing music better than symphonies and carrots better than spinach. She has a repertoire of stories and a wealth of advice, some they appreciate and some they wish she'd keep to herself. Grandma may not be able to give of herself as much as she once did, but her human weakness is itself a gift, helping them develop compassion and tenderness they can use all their lives.

As a parent, you may feel caught in the middle between your children and their grandparent. The challenges come from both sides. My mother-in-law disapproves of some aspects of the way we're raising our children, and she's quick to point out their misbehavior. Sometimes I agree that they are misbehaving, but her intervention pressures me to overreact. Sometimes she's just expressing her own anxieties for them. "Where are you going? How are you getting there? Who will be with you? When are you getting home? Are you sure you're dressed warmly enough? Does your mother know where you're going? Did you lock all the doors?" This puts a strain on her relationship with her grandchildren, who resent all these questions. Often the children are not breaking any of our rules but simply being more energetic than she likes or more outspoken than her children were allowed to be.

It's difficult for me to be both understanding toward Mom and fair to my children. I want them to respect their grandmother and not argue with her — their sense of justice doesn't need nurturing nearly as much as their sense of compassion! I encourage them to give way whenever possible out of consideration for Grandma and to take it up with me later in private.

On the other hand, my children often feel I am showing favoritism or being too easy on Grandma. They point out that she makes a lot of noise when she chews while they must eat quietly, that she doesn't have to finish everything on her plate, that she never has to wash the dishes or take out the trash, that she doesn't apologize if she takes something of theirs without asking.

Welcoming a Parent into Your Home

Again, I try to encourage them to be respectful and understanding, to come to me later with what bothers them rather than openly criticizing Grandma. Sometimes I can shed light on the problem. For example, Grandma's dentures make it difficult for her to chew with her mouth closed. Sometimes I agree with their complaint and decide to approach Mom and try to get her to modify her behavior, although I know it's difficult for an older person to change long-standing habits.

Should grandparents correct or discipline their grandchildren? Briege says yes. "At first it was hard for me when she corrected the children, but I've learned to let her take authority as long as it reinforces the way of life my husband and I have tried to establish. Sometimes we have to talk about the differences in this area."

On the other hand, Nicole had to stop her mother from correcting her grandson. "She was being much too hard on him. He'd come home with an average report card and she'd say, 'I knew you should have studied harder instead of going out to shoot baskets after school. Aren't you ashamed of yourself?' Our son didn't respond angrily, but I could see how much this bothered him.

"I didn't want to confront her directly, so I found another approach. 'You know, Mom,' I said, 'he has two parents telling him what to do. It's our job to discipline him, and we do the best we can. What he really needs is a grandmother who loves him unconditionally, who thinks he's wonderful and often tells him so. You could do him and us a real service by pointing out his strengths; it's so easy for us to zero in on his shortcomings!'"

What if Grandma's orders contradict what you've told your children? Usually it's not the major directives but differences in small things that confuse children. They know you're in charge of setting the rules for them, yet Grandma is an adult so they don't want to disregard what she says or be disrespectful to her. It's particularly difficult when you've left a child in charge.

Sometimes I go out to do an errand and leave an older child in charge of a younger one. I try to make that clear, but Grandma still feels responsible when I'm not there. She often challenges the child's authority. Before long, both are angry.

The first time this happened, I took the baby-sitter aside

and told her that I had indeed put her in charge and was holding her responsible for her younger sister. However, I urged her to do what Grandma wanted whenever she could, unless that would endanger her sister. I told her to do it Grandma's way, rather than arguing, then take it up with me later.

When the children do bring a dispute to us, sometimes we go back to Grandma and tell her it's fine for the children to do a particular thing. They're old enough to get their own snacks out of the refrigerator, for example. Sometimes we modify our rules out of consideration for her. There's nothing objectively wrong with their listening to popular music on the radio, but if it annoys Grandma they should refrain from doing it in her presence. What they are learning about being considerate of others and about working through disagreements is well worth any temporary confusion.

It's a wonderful privilege to be able to share a home with an aging parent. One family affirms this by celebrating the yearly anniversary of the day mom moved in with them. They try to be lavish with affection and frequently tell her how pleased they are to have her with them. It's impossible to say "I love you" too often!

CHAPTER SEVEN

Caring for a Parent In Other Living Situations

In the Parent's Own Home

Even if your mother has decided to live independently, she will still need your support and encouragement. Talk with her regularly about how things are going, and discuss what options she would consider if living alone ever became impossible or undesirable.

What kind of help does she need to remain on her own? Once you identify the needs, seek out sources of help, paid and volunteer. How much can nearby family members do? How often can out-of-town family members come to help? What services are available in her local community?

Mom may need help with housework, especially yardwork, heavy cleaning and repairs. Other needs may include transportation, meals, personal care and more skilled nursing care.

Perhaps family members can take over things like yardwork, home maintenance and repairs, with or without pay. Perhaps someone from outside the family can be hired to perform such services.

When your mother can't drive anymore, she may have to learn to use public transportation. In many places specialized vehicles pick up elderly or handicapped people.

Meals on Wheels provides a valuable service at reasonable cost, delivering one hot meal every weekday to those who cannot provide one for themselves. People can be hired to do housekeeping and to help with personal care such as bathing.

Even if many of these services are available on a volunteer basis, Mom may prefer to pay for them rather than receiving something for nothing. Pam's mother found some good ways to repay her friends.

"Mom can pay for some things, and she's worked out creative exchanges for others. She keeps the neighbor who mows her lawn supplied with cookies. She has a prayer list taped to her refrigerator. Whenever people help, she asks if they have specific concerns she can add to this list; she prays faithfully for everything on the list. She also remembers to ask about needs. 'Is your daughter still sick?' 'Has your co-worker been able to quit smoking?' Prayer may not seem like payment, but it's a real gift she gives others."

Visiting Nurses and many other organizations provide more specialized nursing care. Medicare certifies over 5,000 home health agencies, and home health care is the fastest-growing segment of medical care in the U.S. Two million Americans receive home treatment every year, ranging from round-the-clock care to occasional visits. Most health insurance will cover at least a portion of such services, which cost far less than institutional care.

Many hospitals have services for the homebound, such as telephoning regularly to make sure they are all right, providing monitors or alarms they can use if they can't reach a telephone. Such devices can be very reassuring to both you and your parent.

Nursing care, even unskilled care, is expensive. It's also somewhat risky to bring a stranger into one's home. Horror stories abound about aides who have robbed, defrauded or even molested their employers. Be sure to check references carefully and take normal precautions such as putting cash and valuables in a safety deposit box. A personal interview is also crucial. An aide may be very skilled at nursing tasks, but if your parent doesn't like or trust her or if she doesn't have patience or act with courtesy then the experience will not be a happy one.

A Parent in Other Living Situations

Before hiring someone, have her come for a trial run. Leave a list of duties such as preparing a meal, then ask your parent how well she did, both in terms of results and attitude.

Older people living alone can easily fall prey to swindlers and moochers. Here is Charlotte's story.

"People kept taking advantage of my mother. A man came to her house and told her she needed a hearing aid, but when I took her to the doctor he said she could hear fine! She had a hard time getting her money back; she always likes to pay for things in advance rather than go into debt.

"Then she befriended a man who said he was a Christian and would do work around the house for her. At first he didn't charge much, but one day he told her the Lord said he should charge her $200 for a couple hours' work! Finally she told him she couldn't afford his bills, but she was in a bind because she really needed the work done. Then he began borrowing money from her, and she had a terrible time getting it back. Yet she would loan him more the next time he asked! Finally my husband saw his truck parked outside her house one day, went in and spoke sharply to him. I'm not sure he stopped coming around after that, but at least he knew we were aware of the situation and would look out for her interests."

You may feel that your mother is taking on too much. This is often a source of tension between parent and child. Colleen shares her dilemma.

"I'm afraid that my mother will overexert herself. She's in reasonably good health, but she can't see very well and I'm so afraid she'll fall and hurt herself, or put too much strain on her heart by trying to do too much. I've told her I'd be glad to do things for her, but she doesn't want to inconvenience me. I think it's also important to the way she feels about herself to be able to take care of herself as much as possible rather than to depend on anyone else.

"It doesn't do any good to argue with her. Sometimes she'll listen to her doctor. If I accompany her to a checkup I can ask him specific questions such as whether she should still be going up and down stairs more than once a day. Sometimes his answer surprises me. He feels she's the best judge of what she can handle and knows how to pace herself to conserve her strength.

"We've worked out some organizational helps. She keeps a bag at the top and bottom of each staircase so she doesn't have to run up and down every time she finds one item that belongs on another floor. Gadgets like a long hook to reach high things save her from stretching and climbing.

"After some observation, I wrote down my concerns and discussed them with my husband. We targeted a few things we felt Mom really shouldn't be doing and tried to figure out who could do those things for her. For example, a grandchild who is trying to raise money for a class trip got her to pay for weekly housecleaning. Grandma is really doing her a favor in this way, which makes it easier for her to accept help. The grandchildren have also learned a lot from her about how to do a job right!"

Even with such arrangements in place, you will want to check in regularly with your parent by telephone as well as visiting periodically.

It may be helpful to schedule a regular time to telephone every week or two, a time when the two of you can talk unhurriedly without being interrupted. On the other hand, if overlong conversations are a problem, you may choose to call when some other commitment can signal the end of the conversation, for example, "It's been wonderful visiting with you! Now I have to go pick up the children from school."

Some people find it helpful to keep a notepad by the phone to jot down things that have come up during the conversation which may need follow-up. For example, if she says, "I've been feeling short of breath lately. I really should go see the doctor," next time you call you can ask, "Did you make an appointment with the doctor? Can someone take you? If you tell me when it is, we'll remember to pray for you at that time." If she's concerned about a neighbor, be sure to ask how that neighbor is getting along. Perhaps Mom has asked you to find out something; you want to have an answer next time you call. If you keep track of your conversations in this way, over a period of time you can check on various areas of her life (medical and financial needs, housework, repairs, recreation, friends) without turning each phone call into 20 Questions.

Arlene finds it difficult to converse with her mother, who isn't a very happy person. She says, "Mother likes me to call her

A Parent in Other Living Situations

every week or two, but that's hard for me to do. When I call, I know I'll hear half an hour of complaints and problems, yet she won't want to hear any solutions from me.

"A friend of hers has told me how much Mom looks forward to my calls and visits, so I try to be as faithful as I possibly can. In listening to the same complaints over and over, I've certainly grown in patience!"

An occasional family audio- or videotape, a weekly letter including the kind of newsy details most mothers like to read as well as children's art, schoolwork and programs from special events are all good ways to keep in touch. Some people like to exchange clippings: news about acquaintances, cartoon strips, inspirational pieces or interesting news items.

Each daughter must work out her own rhythm for visiting her mother—frequent short visits or more infrequent longer stays. These are times to help your mother with specific tasks and to assess how things are going for her, but they are primarily times for strengthening the parent-child relationship. Let your mother give most of the clues about what kind of visits work best for her. Between visits, she can put into a shoe box things she'd like you to attend to: bills, correspondence, lists of errands and things that need fixing, for example.

Here is what Priscilla does. "My mother manages all right living alone. This is what she wants, so we try to help her make it work as long as possible. I pray that she'll stay healthy and independent until the Lord takes her home, since that's her desire.

"In order to make it work, I try to spend a day there every week or two. I usually don't stay overnight, since she only lives two hours from me.

"I try not to jump in too quickly. When something comes up, I wait to see how she'll handle it by herself. If I step in too soon, she becomes more passive and doesn't do what she could for herself.

"I see my role as a cheerleader, keeping her spirits up and taking care of emergencies or things she can't quite handle. When there's a special need such as surgery, I stay longer.

"Especially when she's down with an illness or trying to recuperate, I take in freezer meals she can heat as needed.

"Mom is still pretty capable, and what she can't do herself she hires someone else to do. Having a cleaning lady come in once or twice a month is a major concession for her!

"My greatest frustration is lack of time. I often feel torn between things I want to do for my children or grandchildren and things I wish I could do for my mother. Every time I visit, I walk away from things I'd like to do for her. I'm grateful my husband not only encourages me to go but also limits what I offer to do. He reminds me I can't be everything to everyone!

"I take my children and grandchildren to visit frequently, a great blessing for the children and their great-grandmother alike. They're very close."

There is a fine art to making good visits with young children. Megan shares her experience. "Mom couldn't tolerate the children for long at a time. Their noise and energy level quickly got on her nerves, and she was afraid that they might break something in her house.

"When we came to visit her from out of town, we stayed with other relatives and made the children's visits brief, coaching them about things they could do for Grandma or share with her as well as about things they shouldn't do or touch. Rather than always visiting in her home, we planned brief outings where she could relax and enjoy the children without worrying about them. For example, one day we fed stale bread to the pigeons in the park. Mom sat on a park bench while the children played on the swings, occasionally bringing her a dandelion or asking her to watch them perform on the monkey bars."

In a Nursing Home

If your mother is in a nursing home, other people are responsible for her day-to-day care, but you can do a great deal to make sure she receives the best possible care. There are many personal services you can provide for her. More important, she will need a great deal of emotional support from you.

Speaking of her mother, who could not talk after a series of strokes, Sarah says, "I became Mom's advocate. I think I would

A Parent in Other Living Situations

have been her advocate even if she had been able to speak for herself.

"I tried to visit the nursing home frequently, at different times of the day, and sometimes for extended periods. My visits were unannounced. This enabled me to identify times and ways Mother was being neglected and not given the care she needed. I was able to give various staff members suggestions about things she wanted and missed."

Sarah learned legal specifics that helped her mother get the best possible care.

"I was upset when I walked into the nursing home unannounced two different times and found Mother alone in the bathroom. I was afraid she might fall and break a bone. When I complained, the supervisor said they couldn't afford enough staff to accompany every patient to the bathroom.

"Through an attorney, I learned that the law in our state forbids leaving a total-care patient like Mom alone in the bathroom. When I pointed this out, the staff found a way to give her better treatment.

"Another state requirement has to do with the ratio of patients to staff; in our state, it is 7:1. When I asked an aide how many patients she was responsible for, I learned that each was routinely assigned 10 patients, a clear violation of the law. Again, pointing this out led to improvements."

Sarah learned to work out other problems diplomatically with staff members.

"At first, my tendency was to be angry and confrontational. I would march up to the head nurse and say, 'Do you know what's going on around here?' No wonder the nurse usually bristled and got defensive!

"I found it more effective to go first to the nurse or aide directly responsible for Mom's care. I tried to be direct and unemotional, to assume that she was doing her best and one of us might simply need more information. I'd say, 'There seems to be a problem here. Can we work it out?' Sometimes after she explained why she was doing things a certain way, I agreed with her. Other times, she just didn't understand the limitations of Mom's physical or mental condition and could work within those once I explained them to her. If talking with her didn't result in a satisfactory solution, I had no choice but to go to her supervisor.

"I viewed myself as part of a team that included my mother, the aides who cared for her, the head nurse and the doctor responsible for writing orders. I wanted us all to work together to give Mom tender loving care."

Some things may be problems for only one resident. However, often they affect many people. At Sarah's suggestion, her mother's nursing home has begun a monthly family forum open to residents and family members. Heads of all the departments — nursing, diet, activities, housekeeping — attend these meetings. Anyone can suggest agenda items. Some are circulated before the meeting, others come up spontaneously.

These meetings are very productive. The staff hear how they're doing in each area and families begin to understand the challenges the staff face in trying to give their parents the best care. Those at the meetings are able to identify problems common to several residents, to understand why they can't all be solved instantaneously, and to see real progress over time. These aren't simply gripe sessions; often a family member suggests how to do something better. Brainstorming frequently improves the initial suggestions.

Sarah gives more details about visiting her mother in the nursing home. "Once a week I made a 'working visit.' Together Mother and I went through her things to see what might be missing, what needed washing or mending, and what supplies I needed to replace. Everyone will have a different list, but Mom liked to have Life-Savers, tissues, cleansing cream, chapstick, sharp nail scissors, powder and body lotion. I checked this list every time. Inevitably, one or two things had been used up or had disappeared from Mom's room. Other residents meant no harm, but some were confused about what was theirs. We locked up special keepsakes like jewelry, but for things like nail files I just kept a spare on hand.

"I also tried to bring in mail from home, newspaper clippings and current copies of her favorite magazines, which she put in the common room after she finished reading them.

"Mom's needs and abilities gradually changed over the years she spent in the nursing home, but I always found these

A Parent in Other Living Situations

longer visits helpful. The things we did together included taking care of her grooming, going for walks down the hall, reading Scripture and praying familiar prayers. I often went with her to visit another resident or took her to the day's activity (a craft, slide show or sing-along). I usually helped her with lunch and got her settled for a nap before leaving."

Sherry, who frequently visits in nursing homes, has several suggestions for making such visits pleasant for everyone.

"When I began visiting Mother in the nursing home, I would bounce up to her, or to other residents, and say brightly, 'And how are you this fine day?' Sometimes I would get a muttered response, occasionally a longer answer than I wanted, but seldom was I greeted in an upbeat way.

"After a while I began trying a different greeting: 'Hello. It's really good to see you.' This didn't require a response and it often prompted a smile, especially if I made it more specific: 'It's so good to see you up out of bed . . . with your hair all done up . . . enjoying the sunshine . . . with a new photo of your grandchildren.' "

Sherry tries to bring a bit of the outdoors into the nursing home. When she walks down the hall with a bouquet of flowers, people reach out to touch and smell them. Even a handful of colored autumn leaves, a bunch of radishes from the garden or icicles interest people. These things not only bring the outdoors into what can be a very confining environment but also stir up happy memories.

If she can't bring an object from nature, she tries to paint a picture with words of the kind of day it is, how the clouds are sailing before the wind, how the hot sun feels on her arm, how things look in the fog.

Children and pets are almost always welcome visitors. Many nursing homes now bring in pets for therapeutic reasons. Of course, some residents dislike a particular kind of animal, or all animals, but many love to pet a dog or cat. Most older people also respond warmly to children, reaching out to touch a baby and being amazingly patient with the energetic movements of an older child.

Sometimes children make better visitors when accompanied by an adult other than their parent, who may be anxious

101

about their behavior. Of course, children need to be taught how to behave in this situation, to use their quiet indoor voices, for example, to look directly at the person so she can hear them, to move slowly.

However, most children make wonderful visitors. Grandparents and great-grandparents love to display children's artwork, look at their collections and hear about their interests. It's also good for children to be able to relate to someone who has all the time in the world just for them.

When the visitor is not a close family member, she may have trouble finding a contact point or something to talk about. Sherry suggests serving the person in a specific way, for example, offering a shampoo or haircut, giving a manicure or a foot massage with rubbing alcohol or oil. Another idea is to read the person something from her night stand, with her permission, of course. Many people have trouble seeing or remembering. Reading them a letter, a card or a passage from the Bible can be a very precious way of serving them.

Besides a visit to the nursing home, it's refreshing for the resident to be able to get out with you, to spend time in your home, to be present for a Thanksgiving meal, to attend an anniversary party, to see plays and school programs. She may also enjoy shopping, going to a concert, or even tagging along on errands if she's able. Such outings prevent her world from closing in on her.

In the Hospital

Although a hospital stay is temporary, it does present problems, which we will consider at this point.

If you live in a different town, you may feel totally helpless while your mother is hospitalized. There's not much you can do either in terms of practical help or moral support, and it's often difficult to get accurate medical information at a distance. Mom may relay what the doctor says, but you aren't there to ask questions about what concerns you.

Sometimes you can arrange for the physician to telephone you at a specific time. If the hospital staff knows the family wants to be supportive even though they are not on the scene,

A Parent in Other Living Situations

they will try to work with family members as closely as possible.

Here's what it was like for Linda when her mother was dying in a hospital out of state.

"It was hard having my mother so far away when she was sick. While she was dying, I was only able to go to be with her twice, for two weeks each time; I couldn't take any more time off my job and other responsibilities. This was frustrating to me, although I'm grateful for the time we had together before she died.

"Because of my nursing background, my dad relied on me to help make decisions about Mom's care and treatment, even about financial arrangements. However, since she was so far away, it was hard for me to get accurate information about her medical condition.

"I called every night and talked with both parents to encourage Mom and support Dad. Both looked forward to my calls."

If your mother is in a hospital in your town, the challenges expand. It can still be difficult to get medical information. Doctors often make their hospital rounds early in the morning. If you're on hand then, you can talk with the doctor directly. Most doctors also set aside time later in the day to return phone calls; this can be arranged through the office.

Having a parent in the hospital is described by most children in one word: exhausting. Linda continues her account of the two-week periods she spent with her mother.

"Caring for my mother wasn't difficult, but it was exhausting. As a nurse, I knew how to make her comfortable and attend to her needs, but doing it wore me down. I often spent the night with her, then tried to cook and do housework for my father during the day. I found myself fatigued and short on patience!

"I learned not to try to do everything myself but to ask for help. It was also important for me to get away occasionally so I could resume my duties refreshed.

"I had to make an effort to include my brother in caring for Mother. He didn't have the same training, but there were many things he could do for her if I suggested them or showed him how.

"The most important way I cared for my mother was just being with her, being available to talk and listen when she felt up to it. I tried to please her in every way I could. This included cleaning the house in the way I knew she'd like.

"What sustained me was the prayer of Christian friends and the assurance that it was God's will for me to be doing just what I was doing."

If your mother is confused—a common by-product of illness—she may need even more support.

When my mother-in-law was hospitalized, the unfamiliar setting made her even more confused. Even though the staff was there to care for her physical needs, she was unable to make those needs known by using the call button, for example. She also needed frequent reassurance and didn't want to be left alone.

It was difficult balancing Mom's needs during this time with the needs of my family, and I became exhausted. Fortunately, other family members were able to take shifts in the hospital with her, and we enlisted friends to do the same.

Spiritual resources were also very important to me. I read and reread scriptural promises about the Lord being our strength. Isaiah 40:28-31 and Matthew 11:28-30 became especially precious to me. As I tried to listen to Jesus' invitation to come to him and learn of him, I felt him instructing me that a yoke is easy to bear if it's accepted joyfully, but very irritating if I chafe under it. I found that I could truly do all things through Christ who strengthens me (Ph. 4:13) and with the help of the "angels" (other Christians) he sent to help me.

If your mother is confused, she may not understand why she's in the hospital and may become very angry about this. If you're spending the most time with her, the blame quite naturally falls on you. Try to exercise detachment, trusting that you are acting in your mother's best interest and refusing to take criticism personally.

You can learn a great deal by asking staff members questions. Often nurses, aides and therapists are more helpful than busy doctors. Tina says, "Even when he was in the hospital, I

A Parent in Other Living Situations

didn't realize how ill my father was. The doctor thought he'd explained everything to me, but I don't think he ever told me my Dad wasn't likely to come out of his coma. So when I asked a nurse if they were going to put him on a kidney machine, she gave me a strange look and asked if I wanted to talk to the resident. He's the one who told me Dad had brain damage and probably wouldn't recover."

Nurses can share many helpful tips about caring for a person with a particular illness. A social worker will help you make a plan for follow-up care once your parent is released from the hospital. Don't overlook the chaplain as a resource, either.

CHAPTER EIGHT

Caring for a Parent With Disabilities

Stroke

A stroke, also known as cerebrovascular accident (CVA), is brain damage which occurs when something stops the flow of blood to the brain. A blood vessel in the brain can burst; more commonly, fatty substances gradually build up in these vessels or a blood clot (embolism) lodges there. With blood cut off, sections of brain tissue quickly deteriorate or die. This causes parts of the body controlled by these sections of the brain to become paralyzed. Often only one side of the body is affected. Besides paralyzing limbs, a stroke can affect speech or comprehension, bladder control, vision, breathing and swallowing. Muscles may become rigidly flexed.

When an aneurysm (a ballooning dilatation or bulge in a blood vessel) occurs in the brain, it can lead to a stroke. Sometimes this affects the victim's ability to understand, to speak, to walk; sometimes it affects her ability to express ideas. If the person acts as if she understands even though she does not, it can be very difficult to communicate with her!

High blood pressure and hardening of the arteries (arteriosclerosis) predispose a person to strokes. Preventive measures include cutting down on cholesterol and saturated fats and cutting out smoking. There are also medications designed to lower blood pressure.

Damage is not necessarily permanent. Aggressive therapy, especially in the first six months after a stroke, often helps a patient recover such functions as speech and use of her limbs. Different people experience different results from the same therapy; some recover fully, others partially, some very little at all.

Here is Sarah's account of what happened after her mother's stroke. Her family put their mother into a nursing home so she could receive more thorough care, but they remained very involved with her there. She did not recover most of the functions affected by her stroke and died several years later.

"Mom's stroke affected her speech, movement and strength on her right side. We explored every avenue of service and support: physical therapy, occupational therapy, speech therapy. We found some professionals more knowledgeable, helpful and aggressive than others. Some wrote Mom off because of her age and the severity of her stroke, while others were willing to work with her though the prognosis seemed poor.

"We asked questions until we found people who could explain what had happened to Mom, what was likely to happen and what we could do about it. An internist and a social worker were particularly helpful to us. Pamphlets helped some, but every stroke patient reacts differently. We had to take it a day at a time.

"After this kind of stroke, it's very hard for the patient to learn new things. Mom made little progress in physical therapy, but having someone work with her limbs kept her from losing ground; a brace helped steady her.

"I knew she had done some painting as a young woman, so I often took her to the crafts room. With my help, she was able to be very creative. The end results weren't polished, but they are very beautiful to me because I saw how hard she tried and how she put her heart into what she did.

"I also knew she had good taste in home decorating, so I asked her advice whenever we undertook a project such as upholstering or wallpapering.

"Of course, we had to handle her financial affairs. We tried

A Parent with Disabilities

to inform her and consult her before making any big decisions or changes (for instance, putting her house up for sale). She wanted to know who was doing what, and how everything was being taken care of.

"Mom clearly understood everything that was said to her, but she could only say one sentence: 'I love you!' She used it often and appropriately! Her thoughts were as clear as ever, but the stroke had damaged the connection between thought and speech so she wasn't able to say what she was thinking.

"Although Mom never recovered her ability to speak, she was eager to receive speech therapy. She gained confidence in expressing herself through her facial expressions and gestures. It took us awhile to figure out what she was trying to say, but usually we could get at least a general idea, and that helped bring her out of depression and withdrawal.

"Her inability to communicate was very frustrating to her. I tried to turn things around by saying, 'Mother, I'm trying to understand. Please be patient with me, I'm slow today!'

"For example, she'd rub her finger over her teeth after I brushed them. Sometimes I'd say impatiently, 'Mother, your teeth are clean, I just brushed them!' After several months, I finally figured out that she wanted her teeth flossed! I deeply regret my impatience with her. That must have hurt her when she was already feeling so frustrated at not being able to communicate her needs!

"I found that one long visit was better than several short ones. It took me awhile to slow down to her pace, and it took her time to communicate.

"I tried to keep up familiar routines. Dressing carefully and grooming were still important to her. She was keenly aware of being a temple of the Holy Spirit, and she wanted to keep her temple in good order! During my weekly visits, I would take care of her small grooming needs, as well as set her hair and give her a manicure.

"She was self-conscious about her facial expression and inability to speak, but it was important for her to go out. I tried to help her gain confidence by having a positive attitude myself, focusing on the fun of the outing—the food, the shopping, whatever it was—rather than on her difficulties.

"We brought her home for parties and holidays. Before other guests arrived, she'd get settled by the door and serve as our greeter, holding her arms open wide to welcome friends and strangers alike.

"With our encouragement, friends and family members learned to include her in the conversation even though she couldn't speak, to reminisce with her about shared experiences. If they visited her in pairs, they could converse with each other instead of feeling awkward not hearing any response from Mom, yet she could be very much a part of the conversation.

"It was a great victory for her to attend her granddaughter's wedding. It took a year of planning and she had to have a nurse along, but she was able to stay for the whole event, even the reception. Friends at the nursing home learned of her plans, and they became excited for her and helped build her confidence that she could do it.

"I found I needed support, too. It was very helpful to go out to lunch with a friend periodically and talk things over.

"At first it was hard for me to accept the stroke, to believe God would bring good out of it, to believe that he loved Mom and was still close to her.

"Mom didn't seem to be held back by doubts like mine. She entered into Christ's suffering, and I know she prayed for others rather than dwelling on her own problems. I often asked her to pray for my needs and reminded her to pray for those around her in the nursing home.

"I saw her grow in patient endurance, humility and acceptance. She wanted to please her heavenly Father, so she did everything with love and great care for those around her. Accepting her limitations was her spiritual challenge.

"We viewed her stroke not as something that had happened to her but as a challenge to both of us. We both had to pray, be patient with each other, help each other, support each other. Our relationship changed because we couldn't communicate the way we used to, but we learned new ways to communicate."

Alcoholism

Researchers and therapists disagree about the physiological and emotional causes of alcoholism, but one thing is clear: there is no cure until an alcoholic admits her problem, takes responsibility for her poor choices and surrenders to a higher power. Family members may be able to help her come to this point, but they cannot make the decision for her or force it on her. Nor can they prevent her from drinking if she is determined to continue. Alcoholics Anonymous is not only very helpful for an alcoholic but also has wonderful support groups for children of alcoholics.

Two families share their experience with alcoholic parents. Rhea says, "We committed Dad to an alcoholism treatment facility, but at a certain point he had to decide for himself whether to stick with the program. He decided to try, but as soon as he returned home he resumed drinking.

"Once he made the decision to move in with us, however, we began to see a marked improvement. At first we tried to avoid serving alcohol or having it in the house. When we did have it, we kept it locked up. Even this didn't always work!

"Rather than dealing directly with alcoholism, we've tried to meet the emotional needs that contributed to it. As he's received love and affirmation and seen himself as a valued part of the family rather than isolated and lonely, his need for strong drink decreased, then disappeared."

Lorraine had to deal firmly with her mother's drinking because it was endangering her son.

"Our son is old enough to be left on his own in the evening when we go out, but leaving him with his grandmother turned out to be a different story. One evening we returned to find she had passed out from drinking too much! Needless to say, I was angry and upset.

"It was no use talking with her right then. I simply put her to bed as gently as possible. Next morning, however, we had a long conversation. I told her that her actions had damaged our relationship and abused our trust, and that we had to talk about it.

"At first she wouldn't admit she had done anything wrong.

111

She said she didn't start drinking until our son had gone to bed and that her actions hadn't harmed him.

"This didn't satisfy me. I asked her what if our son got up and found her that way; how would that have affected him? What if an important phone call had come in and she had listened to the information but was unable to recall it? What would have happened if a fire had started and our son was unable to help her out of the house?

"I told her we could not leave her with our son until she earned our trust again. In the meantime, one of us would stay home, or we would take him with us or arrange for him to go to a friend's house.

"This confrontation seemed to help Mom face up to her drinking problem and its consequences. She began attending AA meetings, and she hasn't had a drink for over a year."

Hearing Loss

This common ailment can be very hard on you as well as your parent. Hearing aids alleviate many forms of hearing loss, but many older people don't like to wear them, not just because of embarrassment but because they are uncomfortable and can also produce whistling, humming or magnification of background noise. All these problems, actual or feared, should be discussed with a hearing specialist. Of course, the final decision is up to your parent. There is no point in investing in a device she won't wear, even though you may feel it's pointless for her to continue to suffer from something that could be corrected!

People who can't hear well may stop going to church and other public places and especially to social gatherings where the general hubbub makes it difficult to focus on a single voice. Some churches have special facilities for those with hearing impairments, and it's usually easier for the person to hear from certain spots in a room. Patiently explore these options with your parent.

It's hard having to backtrack in conversation and repeat things a person who hears poorly has missed or misunderstood. It's hard on her, too. She wonders if she's understood correctly,

A Parent with Disabilities

and she feels left out when people don't make an effort to include her in the conversation.

Try to change any habits that cause difficulty for a hearing-impaired person: muttering, speaking too rapidly, covering your mouth with your hands and turning away when you speak. Ask your mother to remind you when you forget.

Try to remember that this is more frustrating for her than for you and that she isn't being obtuse. She is keenly interested in what you have to say, but sometimes she gets tired of asking you to repeat things. Be careful not to misinterpret her actions. Most of the time she isn't interrupting out of discourtesy but because she couldn't tell that someone else was already speaking. When she says something that seems like a non sequitur, it's usually because she couldn't hear the last thing that was said.

Mental Illness

Within the scope of this book, we can't deal in any detail with mental illness. If your mother receives this diagnosis, you should talk at length with her physician. Find out about the symptoms and treatment of her particular disease, especially about how your parent is likely to react to things you say and do and about how you can reinforce the therapy she is receiving. In this chapter, we'll talk about some common tendencies bordering on mental illness which call for wisdom and love from children. Depression has already been discussed in Chapter Two. Here we will give some general advice and discuss paranoia.

Children often hesitate to take in a parent with a history of mental illness, and with good reason. Caring for such a person can be very demanding emotionally and physically. If family relationships are already strained, adding a person with serious problems can be the last straw.

On the other hand, there are few ideal solutions for mental patients. Residential treatment facilities are expensive and not very effective in rehabilitating patients. In many custodial arrangements, the atmosphere is depressing. Residents are often poorly supervised and may wander away or endanger themselves in other ways. At the other extreme, patients may be so restricted that they are miserable. Finally, being surrounded with others who have emotional problems is itself not healthy for a person.

With such unhappy alternatives, care within your family may be a better choice. Professionals may have more knowledge, but what these patients often need more is unconditional love. If you are loving and willing to learn, you should at least consider taking your mother into your home.

People with mental illness are usually unstable and inconsistent. It's challenging to love them as they are, deal with them consistently and stick to commitments both parties have made.

Denise says, "Things were not working out well for Mom in her previous living situation, and she really wanted to be closer to all her grandchildren. However, we foresaw several problems and tried to spell out our rules as clearly as possible before she moved in. She had to understand that my husband is the head of the household. She had to be accountable to us for her comings and goings. She had to limit her smoking to certain areas of the house.

"She was so eager to be with us, she gladly agreed to all these restrictions. However, she hadn't been with us very long before she began to forget or defy our terms. We couldn't reason with her, and she resisted our attempts to get her into counseling. Before long, her behavior became dangerous to herself and all of us. After she deliberately set fire to a curtain, we knew we had to insist on professional help. We took her to the psychiatric ward of our local hospital, and eventually she had to be institutionalized.

"After we moved Mom into a nursing home, we promised she could spend the weekends with us. Because of our busy lives, sometimes she spent the whole weekend, sometimes we just picked her up for church and brunch. However, the biggest challenge to our commitment came not from our busy schedule but from Mom's instability. Some weekends she was a delightful visitor, entering into the life of the family with gusto. At other times she was depressed and withdrawn or cranky and critical. We tried to welcome her warmly even at those times, realizing she needed our love even more then.

"She wasn't a fairy-tale grandmother, but all our children

A Parent with Disabilities

learned to accept her as she was. However she was feeling or acting, she was their grandma and they treated her with respect and consideration. We all grew a great deal by reaching out to her in love when she wasn't being especially loveable. We had to rely on Christ's constant love for us and for her. Amazingly, now that she has died, the children remember her very fondly."

Older people, especially those with memory loss, often accuse others of taking their things or plotting to harm them. It's pointless to argue with such a person about the facts. ("Come on, Mom, who would steal your rolling pin?") However, with a sympathetic approach she can sometimes be brought to see things differently. "I know you're upset that you can't find your rolling pin. You know what I think happened? You put it in a safe place and forgot where! Let's look around and see if we can find it."

Besides this kind of gentle reasoning, it's also a good idea to check on her medications. Taking too much or too little of certain medicines can make a person more irritable, forgetful or irrational.

Suzanne tells how her family dealt with her mother's paranoid tendencies. "Mom kept accusing people of taking her things. She seemed to believe that family members were trying to harm her and didn't care about her.

"At first this pulled our family apart. When my sister Candace telephoned from out of town, Mom would give her an earful about all the terrible things I had done to her. I tried to explain what had really happened, but I could tell Candace was beginning to distrust me.

"Then Candace came for a visit. Mom needed a new coat, and Candace offered to take her shopping. Mom had a hard time deciding on a coat, but Candace was patient and helpful. When they finally got home, Mom pulled her new coat out of its box and hurled it on the floor. 'You switched coats on me,' she told Candace. 'This isn't the coat I picked out!'

"There was no reasoning with Mom; she wouldn't accept Candace's version of what had happened in the store.

"Mom's mistrust hasn't changed, but it no longer drives a wedge between me and Candace. Candace refuses to listen to accusations about me; she tells Mom firmly, 'I know Suzanne is doing what's best for you.' "

Alzheimer's

Alzheimer's disease is a progressive, incurable illness that afflicts over two million American adults. Its symptoms include memory loss, confusion, difficulty in reasoning and in performing familiar tasks. No one knows what causes it, but it is not simply the normal aging process. Something organic causes brain cells to become deformed and die.

At present, there is no decisive test for Alzheimer's. A physician will run a series of tests to eliminate other illnesses with similar symptoms, some of which are curable. If there is no other explanation, the person is probably suffering from Alzheimer's.

There is a cluster of symptoms associated with Alzheimer's, but every person won't manifest every symptom. Problems usually begin long before family members who don't live with the person notice them. The older person may be troubled at being forgetful, for example, and devise elaborate schemes to hide this or compensate for it.

Gwen gives an example. "One of Mom's early symptoms was anxiety about details. Before making a trip, she would call the airline repeatedly to confirm her flight. She became a stickler for details, writing people notes explaining things they had always done the same way. She worried constantly about not having enough money, hesitating over writing a $40 check for groceries when she actually had several thousand dollars in her checking account."

Often the first indication of trouble is a shortened attention span and difficulty remembering things. While long-term memories may remain intact for a while, the person can't remember where she keeps the toothpaste, whether she ate breakfast or what someone just said to her. When she asks the same question repeatedly, she is not doing it to be annoying; she has simply forgotten what you told her. Try to repeat the answer in the same words without any more annoyance than you show when the dishes are dirtied again after you wash them!

A Parent with Disabilities

If you ask the person an open-ended question (one that doesn't have a "yes" or "no" answer) to which she can't remember the correct answer, she may make up an answer or accuse the questioner. This is not the same as deliberate lying. For example, a person may reason something like this: "I don't remember what I had for breakfast, therefore I didn't eat breakfast. They never feed me here; I need to go home!"

Forgetfulness generates fear. Paula says, "Mom is basically a pleasant, grateful person, but as her short-term memory has failed she's become much more fearful and dependent on me. She doesn't want me to go anywhere, even upstairs. I know she isn't trying to be difficult, she just has no realistic sense of time. A minute's absence seems like hours to her, and she can't remember where I told her I was going.

"It's hard having her so emotionally dependent on me. I like to remember her as she was and look for the 'old Mom' in what's still left. She never used to demand my attention, so I know she doesn't really want to be this way.

"I've found others to stay with her so I can take vacations with my family and have some regular time out of the house. At first I felt guilty about leaving her, but I know I have to balance her needs, my own needs and the needs of others, especially my family.

"When I leave for vacation, she's extremely upset, which makes it hard for me to leave. However, her caretakers tell me that, once I leave, she settles in beautifully. The nice thing is that when I return she forgets that I was ever gone!"

Alzheimer's usually affects the person's ability to make and carry out plans, learn new things, adapt to new situations, solve problems and foresee consequences. This makes the world confusing and unpredictable! A complex action such as preparing a meal or even getting dressed becomes impossible for her. Rather than admit she doesn't know how to do it, she will usually refuse to try. However, if you break the task down into small steps and give her specific cues, she may be more willing. For example, instead of saying, "Get dressed," hold her blouse up so she can easily see where to put her arms, then direct her to button the buttons. Appropriate actions can often be trig-

You and Your Aging Parent

gered automatically, by handing her a broom or a dishtowel, for example.

Everyone needs opportunities to do meaningful, helpful things. Besides those already mentioned, someone with Alzheimer's may enjoy winding yarn, raking leaves, dusting, stringing beads, polishing silver, folding laundry, sorting things, cutting out biscuits, peeling carrots, playing catch and singing familiar songs. Good activities are simple, repetitive, rhythmic, predictable and engaging rather than novel, complex, expressive or passive.

Choices usually confuse a person with Alzheimer's. Every decision is agonizing for her, yet she resents being treated like a child with everything done for her. I try to structure Mom's life so she can count on a regular routine. She doesn't have to decide whether to get up or eat lunch or take a bath; these things are dictated by the clock or the calendar.

I leave her alone, giving her space to do as much as possible for herself, but I stay within earshot so I can help if she becomes frustrated and can't manage a task.

I give her limited but genuine choices. She may select a book or a magazine, but I don't give her a whole stack of books. Sometimes I just ask whether or not she would like a cookie. If something would not be a good choice, I don't make it available. For example, I put away her winter clothing in the summer and vice versa. On the other hand, I respect her preferences in things that don't matter and won't harm her.

I am cautious about introducing unfamiliar things. Her dentist, for example, recommended a device that might clean her teeth more effectively, but I didn't think she'd be able to get used to something so different from her toothbrush.

The person with Alzheimer's may have trouble interpreting what she perceives. For example, she may fail to recognize familiar people or objects, lift her feet high to clear a dark spot on the floor, try to squeeze through a narrow space or trip over furniture. She may not be able to distinguish a gentle touch from a rough one.

Language may be affected in several ways. Often the person cannot find the right word. She may substitute a similar word or use a circumlocution, for example, "the thing you cut

A Parent with Disabilities

with" instead of "knife." It becomes difficult for her to understand abstract or complex language—"abstract" being anything she can't see or touch at the moment. Even "Please make me a cup of tea" is an abstract command if she isn't looking at a stove, a cup and a tea kettle.

A therapist who has worked extensively with these patients asserts, "Nobody says things that make no sense at all. They have meaning for her, but sometimes it takes a detective to discover the meaning; her words are usually the least important clue." When this therapist can't figure out what someone means, she asks, "Is it very important for me to understand this right now?" Usually the speaker will say no, but if she says it's important the therapist asks yes-no questions in an attempt to understand.

Music is a wonderful gift for Alzheimer's patients, and for the whole family. We have found that classical music and hymns really lift Mom's spirits. She also likes to tune in the evening radio program where the disc jockey plays Big Band music. This brings back happy memories of days when she and Dad used to go dancing. Sometimes she even wants to take a few turns around the living room on my husband's arm, or they will dance their way to the dinner table.

I've also been amazed how many songs she remembers: popular songs from her youth, silly songs, rounds, sing-along tunes. If I turn on a tape or sing the first line of something, such as "Daisy, Daisy," she will usually chime in with the rest. Sometimes a particular song will also remind her of some event from the distant past, usually a happy one.

Long after other forms of thinking disappear, a sense of humor remains. Besides understanding humorous words in a song, an Alzheimer's patient can usually respond to slapstick, make and appreciate puns and remember humorous incidents from childhood. One son took advantage of his mother's sense of humor when they went on a walk together. He'd take giant steps or baby steps and his mother imitated him gleefully and unself-consciously.

In some ways caring for a parent with Alzheimer's is like caring for a small child. Like a child, she can't always communicate her needs, she's easily frustrated and she needs close supervision. However, a baby is learning new things and moving toward greater independence every day, while a person with Alzheimer's will become more dependent and less capable as the disease progresses.

I've tried to remember what helped when my children were toddlers. One thing is simply deciding to be with her, to focus attention and energies on this God-given task. A mother can't function very well if she gets resentful every time her child needs to be fed, changed, comforted or redirected!

A mother learns to tune in to her baby, anticipating and understanding the important needs. I've tried to become attuned to Mom in a similar way. A certain gesture or sound may always indicate the same need, for example, a need to use the toilet. This may follow a pretty predictable schedule. When Mom has trouble putting together a sentence, I can often guess what she wants to say from her body language or expression, what's going on around her, what she was saying earlier or my memory of events which seem to have become linked in her mind. Helping her find the right word or complete her thought is much like teaching a toddler to talk.

As with a small child, physical cues and support are often more effective than verbal ones. I hold her hand when it's trembling, put my arm around her when she needs reassurance, guide her hand to the stair railing. I use words to explain what I'm doing or what I want her to do, but the words serve not so much to convey information as to make contact.

Sometimes a person with Alzheimer's paces or engages in repetitive behavior such as banging a spoon. Again, it's important to understand that she's not doing it to annoy you! Someone who paces should have a safe place to walk, perhaps with music. Annoying behavior can often be eliminated by changing the environment (removing the spoon), but it's also important to ask why the person is doing this. Is it simply a sign of boredom? Does it happen around the same time every day, so that you could schedule a daily walk around that time? Does it indicate fear or anxiety? Can things be changed so she feels safer?

If she is intent on doing something stressful or unsafe, try to distract her. This works because her attention span is so short. For example, when a widower insisted on going out to meet his wife, his son didn't argue about the facts. He picked up a magazine and pointed to an ad. "Can you help me, Dad? What color is this car?" The father was delighted to be asked to help and turned his attention to the task.

Despite all these losses and the resulting dependence, emotional and physical, people with Alzheimer's retain important abilities. Dr. A.R. Luria says, "There is little or no hope of any recovery in memory, but a man does not consist of memory alone. He has feeling, will, sensibilities, moral being . . . and it is here that you may find ways to touch him. In the realm of the individual there may be much you can do."

People with Alzheimer's can have strong positive and negative emotions, which are sometimes triggered by a sensory experience such as a particular smell. They still experience pleasure and pain. They are aware of their environment and should never be talked about as if they weren't present. They want and need to communicate. They can give and receive affection. They can hold opinions and offer advice. Many skills and habits remain, including the habit of courtesy. The most withdrawn person often complies with a polite request, says "Thank you" and "You're welcome," and displays appropriate manners in a controlled social situation like a small tea party.

However, as Alzheimer's progresses, your parent may seem to lose her inhibitions. She says what she's thinking or feeling without much regard for the appropriateness of the topic or the sensitivities of those around her. If someone passes gas, for example, she'll remark about it. If she doesn't like what's for supper, she'll not only refuse to eat it but express her dislike emphatically. She doesn't hesitate to scratch an itch or pick her teeth in public.

It's best to ignore most of this behavior rather than calling attention to it by correcting or making fun of it. With a little instruction, children can understand that they should neither imitate such behavior nor blame Grandma for it. They should show courtesy and patience.

Her inner emotional reality is usually more pressing than the circumstances around her, which are often difficult for her to interpret. Imagine how confusing it must be to find yourself sitting somewhere and have no idea where you are, how you

121

got there, what's going to happen next and who these people are who seem to know you!

It often helps to identify and sympathize with the person's feelings instead of challenging the facts she has fastened on. For example, a 90-year-old may be upset because she missed her mother's visit. Instead of insisting that her mother died years ago, you can say, "You really miss your mother, don't you? Let me sit here by the door with you."

Getting an Alzheimer's patient to do what's necessary can be very challenging. In some cases, you may have to modify what you consider necessary. For example, does she really have to wear conventional undergarments or dress for breakfast? What about that daily bath? As Mom reasonably pointed out one time, she doesn't do much to work up a sweat or get herself dirty! Some days I can tell it would just be too much stress for her on top of feeling sick or cold, so my invitation simply lays the groundwork for bathing the next day.

When I — or, preferably, we together — have decided on the necessary minimum, I can usually get her over the hump by using plenty of lead time, some discernment and a dose of humor. There's an art to letting Mom know what we're going to do early enough so she can be prepared but not so early that she becomes anxious about it. Sometimes it helps to appeal to circumstances. "This is a good time for a bath because the kids aren't around to bother us" or "This is my freest day" or "I've got your bath water all ready." A directive ("It's time for your bath") works better than a question ("Are you ready for your bath?"). Showing her what I want, giving nonverbal assistance, breaking down the task into small steps and giving needed help at every step will ease the way. Instead of aligning myself with the problem by confronting Mom with commands, I try to align myself with her in tackling the problem. I agree that it's difficult but I promise to help her get through it.

I try to think of things to share with her during bath time when I am giving her my undivided attention and caring so directly for her personal needs.

We joke together about which of us is the more stubborn, or about being dragged kicking and screaming into the bathroom; that lightens the journey. Other sources of amusement

A Parent with Disabilities

are her crooked toes and my attempts to make her beautiful by setting her hair. She'll make a joke out of her helplessness and dependence by saying, "You know me inside and out."

God also has a wonderful sense of humor; he always knows when I need a little encouragement. One evening at bedtime my husband and I lifted up our intentions for the next day. One of mine was that Mom would agree to take her bath without any hassle. She slept in a little later than usual the next morning, and as I was hanging up a load of laundry I heard her tapping on the inside of her window. "Is this the day I have my bath? Why don't we do it right away before I even get dressed?" That has never happened before or since, and I took it as a gracious answer to prayer.

A person with Alzheimer's may overreact to what seems like a minor inconvenience. Someone will reach across Mom for the salt shaker, for example, and she'll throw her plate on the floor and say, "I give up!" Sometimes she reacts with despair rather than anger, weeping uncontrollably.

When I think back over what preceded such outbursts, I can sometimes understand how frustration built up. Perhaps people kept interrupting one another or speaking too softly for her to hear. Perhaps no one passed her the butter or noticed she needed help cutting her meat. Sometimes, though, the reason for her outburst remains a mystery to me.

Simple courtesy goes a long way in forestalling such reactions. I am trying to teach my children to ask when they want to use something Grandma has been using, even if it's household property, to avoid quarreling and rough play in her presence, to pick up after themselves, and generally to be considerate toward her and accommodating of her need for a peaceful, orderly environment.

If a person with Alzheimer's is taken into a confusing and unfamiliar setting, she may have what's called a catastrophic reaction, for example, screaming, refusing to move or saying loud and inappropriate things. This happens in strange situations, especially complex ones such as being in an airport, or when events unfold too fast for her to comprehend. She feels overloaded when there is too much going on, too much noise, too much movement, too much clutter. At such times she has no control, things are getting away from her, and she can't cope with everything or everyone at once. Since the people she knows, those who take care of her, are usually busy at such times, no one seems to be responding to her needs, expressed or unexpressed. This can be terrifying.

The best treatment is prevention, trying to foresee confusing situations, to simplify them for her as much as possible and to prepare her for them. If an airplane trip is necessary, for example, purchase tickets in advance and allow enough time so she doesn't get caught in a crowd or a long line. Sometimes it helps to give her a specific task to concentrate on, such as keeping track of a small bag.

Not all catastrophic reactions can be foreseen or prevented. When they occur, try to remain calm rather than reacting angrily. This is difficult, since you may be pressed for time! Don't blame yourself or her. This is part of the disease process that she can't help. Try to remove sources of confusion and anger: turn off the radio, restore objects to their normal order, find a quiet corner for her.

Whether she's simply overreacting or having a catastrophic reaction, Mom usually can't answer questions: "What's wrong? What don't you like? What do you want?" I usually have to guess and try to correct anything that might be contributing to her confusion and frustration. It helps to give her a little space. If I move in too soon with questions or even comfort, she'll shoo me away. Perhaps she senses that she has done something inappropriate and is embarrassed by her behavior. Fortunately, she will not remember either the source of the irritation or her outburst very long, so there is no lasting scar. After a few minutes, a hug and soothing words can assure her that everything is all right.

As Alzheimer's progresses, the person often loses control of motor functions. She may shuffle her feet in place for fear of falling and eventually become unable to walk or speak.

However, she's still an important member of the family. One family gathers annually to celebrate their mother's birthday even though she doesn't seem to understand who's there or why. When she first became ill, a granddaughter started a monthly family newsletter that has remained important to

A Parent with Disabilities

everyone. They contribute to a Grandma Award given to a nursing-home staff member every year.

A daughter in this family says, "Here we all were, talking to Mother as though she could hear us and understand what we were saying. Looking back, I could see that we have all been changed. We have moved beyond seeing her disability as a depressing event. Keeping her as part of our family has bonded us together in a special way."

The disease is eventually fatal, whether the patient dies because of the neurological changes Alzheimer's involves or, more commonly, because of complications. She may choke or become malnourished because she can't remember to chew or swallow her food. Getting food down her windpipe can lead to pneumonia. Incontinence may cause urinary tract infections. Poor coordination may result in accidents or falls. When she becomes bedridden, she may develop bedsores which become infected. Unnoticed and left untreated long enough, any of these side-effects can be fatal, though Alzheimer's patients tend to be quite healthy overall.

There are many helpful books and pamphlets about Alzheimer's disease. One which is compassionate, respectful of the older person and extremely practical is *The Thirty-Six Hour Day* by Nancy L. Mace and Peter V. Rabins, M.D. (published by The Johns Hopkins University Press).

Chapter Nine

Dying, Death and Grieving

Death comes individually to each person and is always unexpected, no matter how long the dying process has been.

Sometimes death comes as a surprise: a parent who had been in good health dies in her sleep or meets with an accident. Often, however, it is possible to see death approaching and prepare to meet it with grace and faith.

Perhaps the doctor has said that Mother is likely to die within a certain range of days, weeks or months. How do you greet this news?

First of all, don't take it too literally! The doctor is giving a ballpark figure based on his experience with patients who have similar medical conditions. Your parent is not a statistic and may well surprise the doctor by living longer—or dying sooner!

If at all possible, she should hear what the doctor has said so that she can discuss with him and you exactly what it means and what choices are involved. Decide what and how to tell her, based on your knowledge of her. What would help her most? Some parents are too emotionally unstable to handle the news that their illness is terminal. However, be sure you aren't basing your decision on what you can handle! Perhaps she will be more cooperative if she thinks she will recover, but most dying people suspect the truth and are relieved to be able to face it directly. Don't forget that your ultimate objective is not to make her more comfortable during her last days on earth but to help her prepare for eternity. God will give her — and you — all the grace you need.

Whether or not she has a living will (giving someone the authority to make decisions about medical procedures), the dying person's preferences should be discussed and respected. What does she consider extraordinary measures for prolonging life? Does she want to be resuscitated if she stops breathing? Does she want to be fed intravenously if she becomes unable to take food by mouth? Should she be hospitalized in order to receive aggressive treatment, or would she rather remain at home, where those she knows and loves can simply try to make her comfortable?

What does the rest of the family think about such measures? Things are much more peaceful if the parent herself has made these decisions and everyone agrees to them before the crisis. If she isn't capable of making them herself, agreement among family members is very important.

Although terminal illness should be a time for family members to draw close together around the dying person, it can be a time of great stress and conflict. Perhaps one son hasn't been reconciled with the parent or with other family members. Perhaps for some other reason he can't accept the fact that his mother is about to die. He may be unwilling to spend time with her or may become angry if every measure isn't taken to prolong life. He may blame his parent's condition on the siblings who have been more immediately involved in the parent's care and decisions about that.

Help in such cases is often available from your pastor or through the hospital, which may also have support groups for families of dying patients. If one person is at odds with the rest of the family, you may have to act without his consent to do what is best for the parent. Obviously, this is a very painful decision.

Is she ready to die? Are there unsettled things you can help her resolve, people she longs to see once more, perhaps to speak a word of appreciation or forgiveness? Is she at peace with God and ready to meet him? Does she know he loves her and is

Dying, Death and Grieving

preparing a place for her? Familiar prayers, hymns and Scripture passages can be a great comfort during this time.

When death is very near, nurses, especially those who have worked with many dying patients through Hospice, can give you a realistic idea of what to expect when. Don't be afraid to ask questions. Hospice personnel can tell you which procedures increase comfort and which ones are really not necessary if the dying person finds them irritating. They usually know exactly how to manage medication in order to minimize pain while keeping the person conscious and alert as long as possible. They can also help you find medical supplies and equipment and line up extra caregivers as this becomes necessary.

Many families have decided someone should be with Mother constantly while she is dying. If two family members can share a shift, this is a great comfort to all. Close friends, neighbors and church members can also be supportive, either by taking turns watching with you, by praying for specific needs or by providing practical support such as meals, transportation or child-care. Don't hesitate to call on them. People are usually eager to help but feel awkward unless you tell them what they can do.

Here's what Nell said about her family's experience. "When Dad found out he had inoperable cancer, he decided against treatments that might prolong his life a little. He wanted to stay in his own home as long as possible. He would have paid for whatever help was necessary for this to happen, but we knew he'd rather have his children with him as much as possible, so my sisters and I compared schedules and tried to work out a plan. My sister who works full-time was able to come to Dad's after work two days a week and spend those nights with him. Two sisters who live out of town alternated weekends. We each tried to be honest about what we could and couldn't do, and we all assumed each one was doing her fair share, even though we were spending different numbers of hours. We agreed that one sister wasn't in a position emotionally to spend long periods of time alone with Dad, so we tried to have someone else there with her during most of her turn.

"We consulted one another often as Dad's medical situation changed, so that our care could be as consistent as possible. We tried to have our shifts overlap so we could touch base and spend quality time with one another as well as with Dad.

"We did use professional services, especially Hospice and Visiting Nurses. They helped us understand what was going on with Dad and how best to care for him.

"We all look back on the time before Dad died as a very special bonding time, not only with him but among ourselves."

Practical Needs

Many practical arrangements should be settled or at least checked out at this time. It is difficult to make prudent decisions in a hurry after someone has died. If they're made ahead of time, you'll be free to deal with your own reactions to death and to reach out to others who may be less prepared emotionally to accept this death. Comforting them in their loss will help you as well.

Make sure there is a will, and that the person named executor is personally and financially stable. The eldest child or the favorite isn't always the best choice; in some cases an attorney can do a better job.

Other practical preparations for death include purchasing a cemetery lot or checking with the cemetery to update old information, selecting a funeral home, choosing a casket and selecting or purchasing the clothing in which she will be buried. If for some reason these decisions haven't been made ahead of time, minimize stress by getting a friend to help you.

Talk with the hairdresser who usually does her hair and get or give notes about hair color and style. Be sure you know her usual makeup type and color.

Find out what information your state (both the state of death and the state of burial, if different) requires on a death certificate and track it down. This usually includes her parents' full names (including her mother's maiden name), her date and place of birth, her full name, her legal address, her Social Security number, her educational level, her last or usual occupation, whether and when she served in the military, the name of the cemetery, its location (county), mailing address and phone number, and the number of death certificates needed. Death certificates are required for Social Security benefits and by insurance companies and banks, as well as legal agencies and government offices.

Write up the newspaper obituary in advance. This gives you time to verify important events, people and dates in your parent's life. Try to think of details that would honor her and honor the Lord. Ask her also, "What do you want people to remember about you? What has been special about your life?"

Talk within the family and with the dying person, if possible, about the funeral service. Try to find out her favorite hymns, Scripture readings, poems, flowers and other details. The funeral home can keep funeral plans on file for you, along with the obituary and death certificate information. Talk with your parent's pastor, too, about the service. Many churches now make provision for holding the wake in church rather than in a funeral home.

Make a list of names and phone numbers of people to notify at the time of death, including family members, pastors, close friends and funeral homes (there may even be two funeral services if she is buried somewhere other than where she died).

Bedside Support

Being with and caring for a person who is dying are very intense experiences. Sherry advises, "Try to focus on the other person rather than yourself. Reassure her, especially if she's afraid of being alone or of dying. A practical service is to telephone special friends she wants notified that she is close to death. During this preparation time, try to remember that this wonderful life is only a sad little shadow of the life to come."

Especially if her dying is prolonged, you will find yourself feeling very drained. It is important to linger over personal prayer and Scripture reading, to take time off for things that renew and refresh you, and to confide in Christian friends.

It is reassuring to her and comforting to you if you touch her. Washing her down, especially if she is feverish, rubbing her all over with lotion, fluffing pillows so she is more comfortable in bed and simply holding her hand are important forms of touch.

On the other hand, don't hover too much. Both of you need space so that she can let go of life and you can let her go. Sarah says, "I read her the second half of Psalm 45 about the bride going to her bridegroom, sang 'Swing Low, Sweet Chariot' and other favorite hymns and spirituals. I said good-bye and told her we'd be able to carry on, with God's help. Then we were quiet together for a long time."

Gathering as a family at this time is especially precious. The family can reminisce, sharing how grateful they are for the person's life. Realizing she has lived a full life and made a real contribution, and perhaps seeing she can no longer participate in life as fully as she once did, everyone may become more ready and willing to place her in God's hands and let go of her.

As death approaches, the dying person may change in ways that are difficult for the family to understand. It helps to realize that God is inviting her gradually to loosen her hold on this life so she can lay hold of eternal life.

Linda's mother had brain and lung cancer. Linda says, "As the cancer progressed, she became more dependent on my father and me. Of course, she also became less active. I saw her grow in patience, faith and kindness. Later on, though, she couldn't reason clearly; she needed frequent reassurance as she became fearful or confused."

Dolores's mother struggled for 10 years with emphysema, diabetes and heart trouble. She lost her central vision. Yet, at age 72, she received her associate degree in library science from a local university, then worked part-time at a library! Dolores says, "As Mom became more ill, she became housebound and dependent. For the last three months, she couldn't even concentrate on the talking books she loved so much. In her last month, she had episodes when she couldn't tell what was real. We all had a hard time with this! Toward the end she vacillated between the person we all knew, loved and respected and a person who was more demanding and at times paranoid and critical. When she seemed disoriented regarding time and place, it comforted me to imagine her becoming oriented to a whole different mode of reality."

Nell had a very hard time accepting changes like these in her father. "Eventually cancer began affecting his brain. At first, we were his darling daughters caring for him so generously and lovingly; later, we became strangers trying to harm him! I knew he couldn't help these personality changes, so I didn't usually lash out at him in return, but there were times when I became very angry with God. Here we were, doing our best to do the right thing for our father, and he was so sick he not only failed to appreciate what we were doing but even twisted it into its opposite! How could God let this go on so long?

"I never got an answer to this question, but I was able to place Dad in God's hands again, to let him work out his own purposes in Dad's life and in mine. I often prayed Christ's words, 'Father, forgive them, for they know not what they do.' When I felt most misunderstood I tried to draw closer to Jesus, the Son of Man, whose perfect love was so thoroughly misunderstood. I knew my love was far from perfect, so I begged God to purify it during this intensely painful time, to let me and Dad both experience the richness of his forgiveness and mercy."

Facing the Reality of Death

Sometimes a romantic notion of the ideal death makes it difficult to accept the reality of the death God seems to have chosen for this person.

Jacqueline confesses, "I had a picture of how my mother should die: fully conscious, surrounded by all her children, breathing a prayer. Others may have different pictures, like a parent slipping away in her sleep or dying unexpectedly. Pain seldom plays a part in our idealized expectations!

"As my mother lay dying, I had to let go of my notions and try to see what God was actually asking of her. I began to see that he was giving her the grace to die right, and to cooperate with that grace rather than imposing my standards and expectations."

When death finally comes, your reactions may be different from what you'd imagined. Sarah says, "Everything I had learned working as a hospital chaplain flew out the window when my mother died! As expected as her death was, it was still a shock to me."

It was even harder for Molly, who was never close to her

father. Although she had been on her own for years, her father's death left her feeling very insecure. She says, "I felt like a significant chunk of what had always stood for stability in my life had suddenly been pulled away—'suddenly,' no matter how long I'd been expecting it!"

Linda was surprised by the guilt she felt. "After Mom's death, I was assailed with many 'I should have . . . ' thoughts and self-recriminations. Of course, I didn't abuse my mother in any way and she often said how good I was to her, but after she was gone I seemed to remember most when I'd been tired or cross and not as loving as I wanted to be.

"The Hospice support group and its literature helped me understand that my reactions were normal, not bizarre."

Take time to let the reality sink in. If possible, linger in the room for a while before rushing to make practical arrangements. Sarah continues, "We lingered in Mom's hospital room for half an hour after she died. The nurse cleaned her up but didn't hustle us out. Those moments were so peaceful, like victory after a battle. We sang hymns and shared Scripture. Each family member thanked the Lord for her and for his faithfulness to all of us. We even used the telephone in her room to notify others of her death."

Practical arrangements crowd in all too soon. At the time of death, call the funeral home; if it's after hours, they'll call back, so keep the phone free. Handle this phone call personally.

If your mother is to be buried out of state, you will have to contact two funeral homes. A flat fee includes the necessary embalming and the shipping container. You may have to call the airline to arrange the flight.

After the funeral home has prepared the body, view it before the time set for visiting. Take along lipstick and any other usual makeup. In this way Sarah was able to correct two major errors: somehow her mother's hair color turned out purplish rather than snowy white, and her nails were a garish bright red, a color she never wore.

Contacts with others right after death, and during the wake and funeral, can be awkward. What is there to say to one another?

Hugs cover a lot of ground, but it's also good to share memories of happy, sad and funny times. Some people may want to know details of the last days and her death. Try to see and share these from the perspective of God's faithfulness in answering prayer. Express gratitude for what each person has meant in your life and your mother's.

Although you may be able to manage, this is a good time to accept help from others anyway. Let friends bring in dinner and make appointments at the beauty parlor for the women in the family. Let them plan and host the funeral luncheon. This frees you to give personal attention to the things only you can do, such as greeting those who call to express sympathy. Let others comfort you. Try to be gracious in being needy for as long as your grieving takes.

If your mother spent much time in a hospital or nursing home, you may want to hold a memorial service there in addition to the regular funeral. Sarah's family did this. "Mom had a church funeral, but many nursing-home residents and staff members were unable to attend. We wanted to give them an opportunity to honor her, share memories of her and express their sense of loss.

"People who live and work in nursing homes see death so often it may become matter-of-fact or very depressing. The nursing-home chaplain helped us plan a memorial service there that was full of joy, with upbuilding sharings and lively music.

"We had a punch and cookies reception afterward so people could continue sharing. Many of our friends joined us for this celebration, including quite a few children. They were such a hit with the patients that some of them have returned to visit the nursing home."

The Time of Grieving

Although there is something very personal and private about grief, this can also be a special time for support and friendship. Sarah found that her grief and joy flowed together naturally as others shared stories about her mother. When friends asked to see photographs of her mother shortly after her death, Sarah's initial reaction was, "It's too soon! This will be too painful." However, doing this had the opposite effect. She says, "Looking at pictures from her whole life put her death in perspective for us. Our lives had been so caught up in her illness and death, we had forgotten the full life she had before she became ill. Recapturing this was wonderful."

Grieving takes a long time, and it's different for each person. Gail says, "I'm still not over my mother's death. The first day was easy, but for two or three months I found myself thinking about her every day, missing her. I still feel tender, especially at special times like holidays. I always loved my mother, but my feelings for her grew stronger at the end, when I had the opportunity to care for her."

Linda had a more delayed reaction. "I had so much to do arranging the funeral, getting Dad settled, going through Mom's things, writing notes, that I didn't grieve for my mother much when she died. Six months later it hit me! I began feeling very sad and weepy. Friends reassured me that I wasn't losing it, that this was a very normal reaction and I shouldn't try to suppress my grief."

Sarah tells how her grieving extended over several months. "In the week after the funeral, I resumed my normal life but tried to leave space for long conversations with close friends, about one a day. I called each person to reminisce and to thank that person for specific things done for Mother or for me both before and after her death.

"As time goes on, life gets busier and these precious memories fade. I'm so glad I called people soon after the funeral while those memories were still sharp. I also recorded stories about Mom on a tape which I play every once in a while. I wish I had asked more friends to speak onto the tape.

"It took me six months to write individual notes to everyone, again sharing gratitude for what they had meant to Mom and what they had done for her. I took my time about this, though I worked at it steadily. It, too, provided a natural way for me to grieve. I wept tears of joy over those notes, and tears of loss because I missed her.

"After about a year, I discovered a newfound joy. I had so many happy memories, things that had been temporarily obscured by Mom's long period of suffering. I could look back on her life and see victories, shining like stars, testimonies to God's

Dying, Death and Grieving

faithfulness to her. I realized more fully what it means to say that he is faithful from generation to generation."

Tina mentions two Scripture passages that were especially meaningful to her in her grieving: "We would have you be clear about those who sleep in death, brothers; otherwise you might yield to grief, like those who have no hope. For if we believe that Jesus died and rose, God will bring forth with him from the dead those also who have fallen asleep believing in him" (1 Th. 4:13-14), and Psalm 27:10, "Though my father and mother forsake me, yet will the LORD receive me" (Ps. 27:10). She explains, "Of course, they haven't forsaken me, but they aren't here with me, so the Lord promises he will be with me."

If one parent survives the other, you have his or her grief to deal with as well as your own. Many practical decisions must be made, such as whether to move and what to do with the deceased person's belongings.

You may prefer to have these things settled as soon as possible, but it isn't wise to push the surviving parent or to take over by making decisions yourself or disposing of things before the person has time to retrieve the memories they hold. Fatigue and grief make it hard to reach good decisions, so it's best not to make a major change before the first anniversary of the spouse's death.

A surviving spouse may need a great deal of practical assistance during this time. If your father always paid the bills, for example, or took care of repairs to the house and car, your mother may be bewildered by her new responsibilities, at a time when her own energies are at a low ebb after the work and worry of caring for a dying husband. She may need help notifying all the necessary people, getting life-insurance benefits, organizing bills, sorting through possessions or developing a realistic budget and schedule for herself. Sometimes it's tricky figuring out how much to do for her and how much to let her do for herself, how much to push her and how much to stand by and let her set her own pace.

You cannot force a person to express grief, but you can be alert for warning signs that she has not dealt with it. Molly notes, "After my father's death, we noticed changes in Mom. She used to be a careful, almost perfectionist housekeeper, but

137

now she lets both cleaning and straightening go until it's quite noticeable to others. This has been going on for a year.

"She's also become much more fearful. She doesn't want to move, but living in the house alone is scary for her. Often she can't fall asleep until 2 a.m., then she sleeps until noon or later. She has double locks on all her doors and is very careful to lock screen doors and windows."

Noticing changes like these is one thing; dealing with them is quite another! You cannot force your parent to grieve in a particular way. She will probably resent it if you probe, or if you suggest either that she has resumed normal life too rapidly or is being paralyzed by depression too long.

Try to find occasions to talk about the parent who has died, perhaps by sharing and answering sympathy notes, going through clothing, photographs and other souvenirs. Express how much you miss him or her, in specific terms. "I wish Dad was here to give me advice about whether to repair this car or buy a new one." "Every time I see a shovel, I remember Dad turning over the garden first thing every spring." Be open about your feelings and try to be available if she wants to express hers. If grief seems to be interfering with her ability to take care of herself, her pastor may be able to help her find a support group or professional counseling.

Linda talks about her father's reaction to her mother's death. "Dad didn't even want to go to the funeral home, certainly not to linger there. He hasn't visited the grave and says he doesn't intend to. I haven't tried to push him; he's got to find his own way of grieving. He does sometimes talk with me about Mom and gets teary-eyed occasionally. It's hard on me when he brings up Mom's illness and death, because it stirs up my own emotions, but I think it's important for me to listen when he wants to talk.

"Mom's death left a big hole in his life. While she was dying, I got in the habit of calling to talk with them every night. After she died, he still looked forward to my calls. He wanted to share all the little details of his day with me, the things he used to share with her. My phone bills were pretty high for a while, but I think it was important for me to be available to

Dying, Death and Grieving

him. Gradually he's begun to rebuild his life and develop new friendships and interests."

Going through the dead person's things is a difficult task, not only because they may be numerous but because many have specific meaning and memories attached. If all the children and the surviving spouse are able to do this together, it can be a precious time for sharing memories, especially if the parent has been living in the family home.

If your mother made her home with you during her final days, you can suggest that a different child oversee the disposition of her things. Of course, it will be easier if she communicated her wishes about specific treasures before she died.

CHAPTER TEN

Preparing for My Own Aging and Death

Living with an older person has made me realize a deceptively simple fact: I am growing older, too! In fact, like all human beings, I am moving toward the time when I will be called from this life.

What can I do now to prepare for this? How can I become the sort of old person I want to be, a source of love for others and a joy to those who in their turn will care for me?

On a practical level, I can keep my body, my mind, my affairs, my relationships and my spiritual life in good working order.

I can practice preventive medicine, having the recommended medical tests and checkups, developing a trusting relationship with the doctor responsible for my primary care. I can develop healthy eating habits before a specific medical condition necessitates cutting down on salt, fat and sugar. There is no better time than now to stop smoking or depending on alcohol and excessive medications.

There are many forms of exercise I will be able to continue when I have less energy and agility, such as walking, swimming and playing golf.

What would I still like to do and learn? While my fingers and brain cells may not work as rapidly as they once did, my life experience may make it easier for me to link new knowledge with things I've already mastered. Learning something new can be a great joy. Those who take up new hobbies or remain vitally interested in current events find it easier to sustain a cheerful outlook and to maintain friendships.

Mary Ann, who is 86, testifies, "Since I'm in a wheelchair, I'm dependent on others for transportation, but I keep in touch with old friends by mail, I read, help with housework, sew, type and take continuing-education classes in watercolor painting, business and literature. I'd like to help adults learn to read if I could find transportation. I find I do less necessary work and more hobbies.

"My doctor says I act like a 70-year-old, and I don't feel my age. I have some trouble with my memory, but eventually I can sort things out. I'm still interested in everything, especially current events. I try not to be blue or depressed. If a person keeps in touch with the world and other people of all ages, she won't notice she's getting old."

Setting my own affairs in order includes writing or updating a will, talking through medical preferences with my doctor and family members, perhaps assigning durable power of attorney for medical and financial decisions. Practical preparations for death discussed in the previous chapter should be made for myself and my spouse as well as my parent.

Spouses should share information about household tasks only one has done, whether it's balancing the checkbook, handling investments, doing laundry or keeping addresses current. They should review together their insurance needs and provisions. Retirement is a natural time to review savings, income, budget and needs. They and their children should know where to find important documents and what to do with them after one spouse dies.

It's important to maintain good relationships with friends and family members, quickly reconciling misunderstandings and hurts that may occur. It's healthy psychologically to have friends of different ages. This provides a cushion against the sadness of seeing old friends decline and die. On the other hand, glancing through the address book and noting how many friends have already died helps me gain perspective. Like these

My Own Aging and Death

friends, I'm not indispensable and I won't live forever, at least on this earth! Listening to the wisdom of older people is a wonderful preparation for aging gracefully myself.

The most important preparation for dying is living well today, accepting every opportunity God offers to grow closer to him.

How can I prepare to grow old and die? Mercifully, I can't anticipate everything I'm going to face. All I can do is live each day as fully as possible and as virtuously as possible, to learn as much today as God intends for me to learn. One of the most important lessons I can learn is detachment, to attach myself to nothing but God and his will for me and those I love.

I observe this detachment in my mother-in-law and marvel at it. I can imagine how much detachment it takes to live with one's children: detachment from material possessions, your own routine, life-style and autonomy. When the time comes, I pray I can surrender myself to God's love as wholeheartedly as Mom is doing.

Loving and taking care of my mother-in-law now is part of God's plan for me as well as for her. There is no guarantee that my physical and mental faculties will remain intact, but I never need to lose my ability to give and receive love. The more I practice that now, the better prepared I will be to grow old gracefully.

More books from Greenlawn Press to strengthen you in your Christian walk!

Fathers, Come Home:
A Wake-Up Call for Busy Dads
By Bill Swindell

National family advocate Bill Swindell offers sound father-to-father advice on why we must abandon life in our self-absorbed worlds and begin active parenting. Our kids need—and deserve—nothing less! This book, filled with touching stories and hard-earned wisdom, will be a help to any dad striving to be the father God wants him to be.

$7.95, paper, 101 pp.

For the Bride:
Finding Your Way in the First Years of Marriage
By Ruth Sanford

With keen insight, compassion and candid illustrations from the early years of her own marriage, Mrs. Sanford offers practical help in such areas as communication, romance, prior expectations, sexuality, pregnancy, managing a home, in-laws and the differences between men and women. Ruth Sanford explains how to make these years the beginning of a fulfilling, Christ-centered life together.

$7.95, paper, 136 pp.

To order more copies of **You and Your Aging Parent** please send $10.95 plus the amount listed below for shipping and handling. Please send all orders to:

>Greenlawn Press
>Dept. B1
>107 S. Greenlawn Ave.
>South Bend, IN 46617

Payment must accompany order. Please add 7% for shipping and handling (**$2.00 minimum**). Payment may be by check, money order, Visa or Mastercard. If paying by credit card, please include your credit card number, your name as it appears on the card, the expiration date of your card, your phone number, and your signature on your order.

You can also order by phone using your Visa or Mastercard. Phone us at 219-234-5088 (no collect calls) or fax 219-236-6633 between 8:30 AM and 4:30 PM EST, Monday through Friday.